Homeschool Guide To

The
Internet

Homeschool Guide To

The Internet

Your Roadmap to the Information Superhighway

Mark & Wendy Dinsmore

Foreword by Kathy Ridpath

HOMESCHOOL GUIDE TO
THE INTERNET

© 1996 by Mark & Wendy Dinsmore
Cover design & book layout by Mark & Wendy Dinsmore

ISBN 1-888306-20-3

First Printing October 1996

Published by Homeschool Press
229 South Bridge Street
PO Box 254
Elkton MD 21922-0254

Send requests for information to the above address.

Printed in the United States of America

America Online is a registered service mark of America Online, Inc.
CompuServe is a registered service mark of CompuServe, Inc. Other names used in this
book are trademarks or service marks of their respective holders.

Dedication

✳ ✳ ✳

To my wife, whose labors of love have not only birthed our wonderful son, but have also brought to life this work, our second book together. Thanks, honey, for prevailing over countless calls online, reams of writing and research, and hours of endless editing. Without your encouragement and endurance, this project would never have been more than a sparkle in my eye.

Thanks...

✳ ✳ ✳

To Phillip Hibbard, our Publisher, and the staff of Homeschool Press ♥ To Mary Pride—for your support and the foreword to *Homeschool Guide to The Online World* ♥ To Kathy Ridpath—for your encouragement and the foreword to *Homeschool Guide to The Internet* ♥ To our son Garrison—for giving up time with mommy so she could write books with daddy, finish her degree, and keep a sane mind! ♥ To the Lord Jesus and our Heavenly Father—Creator of Heaven and Earth, in Whose divine providence we experience the wonders and trials of life, and in Whose infinite wisdom established our family and home.

T.Y.C.F.E. ♥ *Y.L.H.C.M.L.*

Contents

Foreword

Mark and Wendy Dinsmore's *Homeschool Guide to the Internet: Your Guide to the Information Superhighway* gives you clear and practical directions as you steer your homeschool onto the Internet and choose from the many "lanes." As you read their book, consider these four areas or "lanes": communication, research, productivity, and fun.

The Internet's communication "lane" is unique, using the written word almost exclusively. This enables us to reach out (sometimes instantly!) to others in a powerful and effective way. One example was the writing of this Foreword. I communicated with Mark & Wendy through electronic mail (or e-mail), the most dominant form of communication on the Internet. Through our e-mails, we introduced each other, relayed our ideas back and forth, and got to know each other better. E-mail brings us closer to one another, giving us an amazing communication tool. Other forms of Internet communication include chat areas, forums, mailing lists, and even voice communication.

Let's switch "lanes" to another important way homeschoolers can utilize the Internet… research!! We use this extraordinary research tool daily in our homeschool pulling down information for unit studies, specific subject areas, and unplanned interests. Not only are we accessing this information from the comfort of our own home, but I've noticed how this consistent use is honing our research skills. I would love to share the many ways we have used the Internet for research; they are just so numerous!

The last two "lanes" I'd like you to consider are productivity and fun. The Internet can help you with tools and ideas for personal productivity. You'll find others sharing hobbies and interests, providing insights and tips, and supplying news and opinions. For example, a quick search online yielded information for our new interest in quilting.

Last of all, don't forget about the fun! Be assured that there are places to visit on the Internet for good, safe entertainment. Just try telling my son it isn't fun to visit websites about cars!! I always "travel" with my children as they venture onto the Internet. Being a discerning and adventurous parent will result in fun and worthwhile Internet "trips."

As you consider the Internet, relax and enjoy it. The Internet is a great addition to any homeschool!! With Mark & Wendy's *Homeschool Guide to the Internet*, you have a map to help find your way onto and around the Internet. I hope you have many rewarding "trips" on the Information Superhighway!!

Kathy Ridpath

Kathy is a wife, homeschool mom, sysop on the Christian Homeschool Forum (on CompuServe's™ Christian Interactive Network) and webmaster of several Internet websites. You can e-mail Kathy at kathy@outrig.com.

Introduction

W hat is that? "http://www.xyzcorp.com"? Virtually unheard of a couple years ago, it is now nearly impossible to turn on the television or read a magazine without seeing an e-mail or Web page address.

If these strings.of.letters.with.no.spaces appear to be strange, cryptic messages to you, we'll help you decipher the code to unlock a whole new universe of information. In our first book, *Homeschool Guide to the Online World,* we introduced readers to the basics of selecting and signing on to an online service as a means to explore the World Wide Web. In *Homeschool Guide to the Internet,* we'll show you how to take full advantage of what is unquestionably the most significant technical, educational, and sociological phenomenon of this decade.

Whether you're a veteran computer user, or have just purchased your first system, the educational opportunities on the information superhighway are abundant. Vast resources are now available to homeschool families. Send mail instantly to family, old friends across the country, and new friends around the world—and never pay for stamps. You can even exchange pictures! Tour virtual museums. Travel to a foreign country. Search the archives of libraries for out-of-print books, or read the latest papers on scientific research.

With the easy-to-read explanations and resources in this book, you'll soon be "hanging ten"on your own keyboard with FTP, Gopher, and USENET.

"Cowa Bunga!"

Mark & Wendy Dinsmore
October 1, 1996

✔ *We've included a few tips in the margin like this one, but the rest of the space is left for you! Keep this guide at your side as you explore the internet and its vast resources. You'll want to mark your favorite sites (and maybe your least favorite too), add your own comments, and write down new links & discoveries.*

Preface

WHAT'S THIS BOOK ALL ABOUT?

This book is a sequel to *Homeschool Guide to The Online World*, which was designed to introduce newcomers to the fastest, most convenient routes to "getting online." While not required reading, the authors' first volume does contain valuable information and advice for the beginner (including more than 150 World Wide Web sites of interest to homeschoolers), most of which is not repeated in this, their second guide.

This new resource features over 250 *more* Internet addresses, including *all-new* Web pages, FTP, Gopher, Usenet, and Mailing-list addresses.The focus of this book is to educate the homeschool community about the larger realm of resources available on the Net, beyond the reaches of online services such as AOL, CompuServe, and Prodigy. Regardless of whether or not you've been online before, however, *Homeschool Guide to the Internet* will introduce you to a whole new world of computing.

WHAT WILL THIS BOOK DO FOR ME?

This book provides an overview of what these other Internet services are, how they work, and what you need to use them. Think of this guide as a "condensed version" of more expensive books that are not dedicated to the needs of homeschool families. While it is beyond the scope of this book to help you install, configure, and use specific online software (the program's documentation can tell you that), you will find many helpful tips, preferences, and definitions to help simplify and demystify the Internet.

The real treasure in this volume is the convenient topical listing of more than 250 Internet resources of interest to homeschool families. This feature alone could save you dozens of hours online. In addition, you'll find family concerns and child safety addressed, as well as an appendix describing Web-browser "plug-ins" to increase your enjoyment of the Internet with state-of-the-art Web design and communications technology.

FOR HIGH-PERFORMANCE READERS

If you are familiar with most of the terminology and already have a few online hours under your belt, you may be ready to skip directly to chapter 7, the "Homeschool Resource Directory." There, you will find more than 250 resources of interest to homeschool families. Otherwise, we trust that you will benefit from overview in chapter 1, as well as explanations of some of the most widely used Internet services in chapters 2-6.

LOAD 'EM UP!

...OR IS THAT "MODEM UP!"

CHAPTER 1

Welcome to the ACME Internet Driving School...

GETTING YOUR COMPUTER onto the Information Superhighway can be a daunting task, particularly when all four lanes are full of technology passing by at the speed of light. Fortunately, you don't need a system capable of keeping up with the "Porsches" and "Ferraris" of computing. All you need is some patience, determination, and encouragement to pave the way for a smooth high-speed merge into this new medium of communication. Hopefully, this guide will help ease your transition from being "mired" to getting "wired."

WHAT IS THE INTERNET?

If the Internet is likened to the entire universe of networked (connected by telecommunications) computers, it is comprised of many smaller (but still very large) "galaxies" of sub-networks. Each galaxy, in turn, is made up of clusters of smaller networks, which ultimately are formed by millions of individual computers. The Internet, therefore, is the physical system of roads or paths which connect all networks and all computers.

There are a number of "vehicles" with which to travel the Web described in this book. Gopher, FTP, Usenet, and Web browsers all provide the means by which to navigate the Internet and transport data. Just like various types of automobiles suit different purposes, so do these "virtual vehicles" on the Internet. Due to its new high-tech appearance and features, the World Wide Web has become the preferred means of conveyance, with which to travel, site-see, and even conduct business on the Internet.

WHO INVENTED THE INTERNET?

The Internet was originally developed in the 1960s by the Department of Defense to ensure the security and continuity of government research by academic and military workers, even in the event of nuclear attack or widespread failure of telecommunications. (Scientists and professors soon found other uses for the Net, however, including personal electronic mail **(e-mail)** and even games.)

Until recently, use of the Net was mostly limited to those with access to large mainframe and mini computers in government and educational institutions, or private corporations. In fact, many users of the Internet took pride in its exclusivity protected by a disjointed array of **USENET** newsgroups, **Gopher, WAIS, Telnet** and e-mail. Finally, a group of scientists from the European Particle Physics Laboratory in Geneva, Switzerland, set out to remedy this situation. The result of their collective efforts, in 1990, was the World Wide Web.

HOW DOES THE INTERNET WORK?

Since computers rely on telephone lines to communicate with each other just as people do, ordinary communications from one location to another would be impossible if the connecting line was disabled. However, by splitting up a single message into several data "packets," computers can distribute parts of one message via several (sometimes many) different routes, all at the same time. This is the equivalent process of the U.S. Postal Service chopping a letter into several fragments, putting each piece on a separate truck, and sending each truck on a different route across town (or across the country) to get to the intended destination, and then reassembling the letter on the doorstep of the recipient.

Fortunately, computers can do this far more quickly and accurately (without any tape and glue) than the hypothetical example above. How? When a message is separated into packets for transmission over the Internet, each packet is "stamped" with the correct address, and a code which tells the receiving computer what order to reassemble the parts to form the complete message.

HOW DO YOU GET CONNECTED, AND WHAT DOES IT COST?

The quickest and simplest means of connecting to the Internet and the World Wide Web still is, for many, to subscribe to a major online service (such as America Online) that includes a Web browser in its free software, then simply follow the directions for installation. You'll get 15 hours of free connect time (not including telephone charges), and then be billed just $9.95 per month for up to 5 hours (300 minutes) of use. Additional time will be billed at $2.95 per hour. While this is a great way to experience the Web for the first time, it's pretty easy to burn up your monthly time allowance with just one research project or even casual browsing; 20 minutes a day for 20 days equals 400 minutes of connect time.

Another route is to buy a prepackaged "Internet starter kit" that includes a book and software (usually on CD-ROM). These packages usually run about $49.95, and generally include an installation program for a nationwide Internet Service Provider (ISP). National or local ISPs generally charge $20 to $25 a month for membership, which generally includes 20 to 100 hours a month (some services provide unlimited access for this fee). Configuring your software will be a little more involved, but the company's technical support staff is generally happy to get you set up. Ironically enough (in our experience) the local ISPs have been more helpful, since they are smaller and more service oriented than nationally-marketed ISPs which can be over-marketed and over-burdened. Check Appendix A for a partial listing of ISPs in your state.

Whether you choose an online service or an ISP for your Internet access, keep in mind that if you live in a metropolitan area, your phone connection will usually be free. Otherwise, long distance charges will apply (on your monthly phone bill) in addition to your subscription fee (generally billed to your credit card each month).

✔ *AOL recently announced a new, lower rate for "power user" subscribers: 20 hours for $20 a month. This is more in line with other local or national ISPs.*

Appendix B lists local ISPs in all 50 states. Simply locate your state, closest area code, and call for information. Getting connected is similar to signing on with any online service: place a call, obtain the terms, and provide billing information.

THE TECHNICAL STUFF

If you've decided to find a local or national ISP (as opposed to an online service), you're ready to install and configure your Internet software to establish an IP (Internet Protocol) account. There are three kinds of IP accounts:

1) PPP (Point to Point Protocol)

2 SLIP (Serial Line Internet working Protocol)

3) CSLIP (Compressed Serial Link Internet Protocol).

PPP is a newer, slightly better version of SLIP. However, both are commonly referred to as SLIP. PPP is generally the connection of choice because it is the standard Internet serial-line (phone line) protocol. Most Windows TCP/IP programs support PPP/SLIP, and include "WinSock" which specifies the needed information for applications to interface with TCP/IP.

The standard Macintosh TCP/IP program, MacTCP, a system extension, comes by itself and does not include PPP/SLIP support (you'll have to obtain "Config PPP", a control panel, through an Internet starter kit or by downloading it from an Internet resources forum in an online service if you already subscribe to one).

To set up a SLIP/PPP connection, you'll need to know some special information. This information should be supplied by your service provider.

• Your IP address—this is your numerical address on the Internet, which you can find out from your ISP. It will look like 123.45.678.901 except with your specific numbers

CHAPTER 1 · WELCOME TO THE ACME INTERNET DRIVING SCHOOL

- Your Netmask—another similar numeric code such as 123.123.123.0

- The IP address of the ISP's computer—it will be like your IP address only with different numbers.

- Your host name: This is your user ID (your online name or ID number).

- The provider's domain name—this the name of your provider, such as compuserve.com.

While this may sound like a lot of unnecessary or complicated nonsense, once you have walked through the steps with your software instructions or your ISP, you will not have to worry about understanding it.

Congratulations—you've passed the test!

✔ *Even though you may never need it, we recommend backing up your Internet "preferences" file(s) once they have been configured. If you are on AOL, this file is called the "Online Database." If your computer ever crashes or these files become corrupted, replacing the damaged files with your backup copy will save you valuable time and frustration. Just copy them to a floppy, and put the diskette away (but not too far away) for later use.*

E-MAIL

THIS ROADSIGN ICON INDICATES AN E-MAIL RESOURCE
IN THE "HOMESCHOOL RESOURCE DIRECTORY" IN CHAPTER 7.

CHAPTER 2

DON'T Wait a Minute, Mr. Postman...

CHAPTER 2

DON'T Wait a Minute, Mr. Postman...

No stamps to lick. No clock to beat, no traffic to fight, and no waiting in line. And best of all, no postage to pay! Sound too good to be true? It's not. **E-mail** (the popular short form of Electronic mail) is a widely used service of the Internet that has become indispensable to many homes and businesses.

With an online service or ISP connection to your home computer, all you need to begin sending and receiving e-mail are two things: 1) an e-mail address

✔ *Our favorite e-mail program is POPMail (shown at left). Eudora is another popular e-mail program that is bundled with many Internet starter kits. You can also download these utilities from the Internet or your online service, free of charge.*

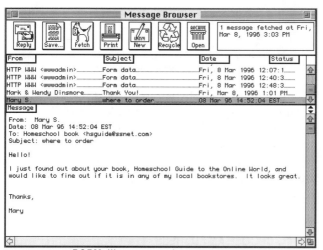

POPMail's message browser screen

(generally created or assigned when you subscribe to an online service), and 2) a mail program (these are usually built in to services such as AOL and CompuServe, but may not be not included with a direct Internet connection. We prefer to use POPMail, shown above.

In addition to text, you can even attach or append sounds and pictures to be sent with your written messages—to any other e-mail address on the planet (we'll show you how later on). The best part is, if your modem is able to connect to the Internet through a local telephone number, then your call is FREE, regardless of what state or what country your message is traveling to. This is a big reason why millions of people are getting "wired up" to the Internet.

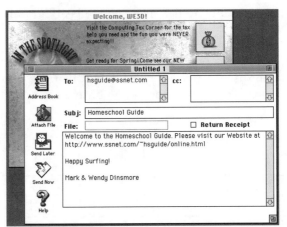

The opening mail screen on AOL

It is quite possible that in the next few years, a significant amount of voice communication will also be transmitted and received via the Internet. Initially, the quality may not be as clear as using the telephone, but even long distance calls will be virtually free! In fact, you can do this now with a microphone and a Netscape browser plug-in (see Appendix C).

HOW TO CHOOSE AN ADDRESS

Each Internet citizen is given (or sometimes able to personally create) a unique e-mail address that identifies them to the rest of the online community, and serves as an electronic P.O. Box address. An e-mail address generally includes the user's screen name (which most services allow you choose) and the host computer's name (which is fixed by the Internet Service Provider), separated by the "@" sign.

CHAPTER 2 · DON'T WAIT A MINUTE, MR. POSTMAN...

It is common for individuals to have several screen names—and therefore several e-mail addresses—for various purposes. For example, our author e-mail address is "hsguide@ssnet.com" and our family e-mail address is "WE3D@aol.com." Depending upon the number of names allowed by your service provider, each member of your family could choose a screen name, or you could divide them up on the basis of work, hobbies, interests, or other affiliations. Consider the CB "handles" of the 70s or the clever 6- or 8-character arrangements of letters and numbers on customized car license plates. Most people use similar creativity in selecting a screen name.

HOW TO GET SET UP

You will need a few things to get started using e-mail: 1) access to the Internet—via an ISP (Internet Service Provider) or an online service, such as America Online or CompuServe, that has a mail gateway to the Internet; 2) an e-mail program—either a stand alone program such as Eudora, POPMail, or one provided with a commercial online service; and 3) the e-mail address of your intended recipient.

Sending e-mail is such a fun, easy process that you may prefer it to the process of composing and sending snail mail (mail sent through the U.S. Postal Service). To send mail, access the "create mail" option by using your specific menu command and a new e-mail form should appear. Fill in the recipient's address, the subject of your communication, and then your message, in their respective fields. Most programs have an address book where you can store the names and e-mail addresses of frequent contacts. Many programs have a time-saving feature that fills in the address field for you when you select a name from your address book.

HOW E-MAIL WORKS

Once you've written your message and mailed it (generally by clicking on the "send" button or typing a keyboard shortcut), it begins its journey to the addressee.

✔ *Most services allow you to "own" more than one screen name, and therefore more than one e-mail address. You don't have to use all of your available names at once, however; keep one or two in reserve that you can assign as your online interests grow, or as younger family members earn the privilege by demonstrating competence and responsibility.*

The "e-message" travels from your computer to your ISP's computer, and from there may travel through hundreds of connections on its way to the recipient's host computer. The recipient's ISP will then send notification to the addressee that they have new mail. The mail is stored on the host computer until it is retrieved, or taken from the "mailbox," at which time the reader can send an instant reply, save the message to a text file, or "shred" (delete) it.

This process, amazingly enough, is generally completed within seconds or minutes. Sometimes, however (depending on what part of the world the message must travel to), your outgoing mail may be delayed several hours as it waits for connecting computers to carry it to its destination.

JOINING A MAILING LIST TO RECEIVE E-MAIL

In addition to receiving mail from friends and family, you can receive mail regularly—from groups with interests like your own. How do you do this? The process is simple: Join one of the thousands of mailing lists available to netizens. Where do you begin? We will give you a head start in choosing one a little later in the Homeschool Resource Directory (Appendix A).

Mailing lists are accessed by e-mail (both subscribing and unsubscribing). Once you have chosen a list to subscribe to a regular influx of mail will arrive at your mailbox daily. Depending on the topic and size of the list you choose this volume of mail could quickly fill your mailbox. We recommend only trying one list at a time and seeing if it is something that you are able to participate in. Subscribing to more than one mailing list can easily become hard to manage.

There are three parts to each mailing list: 1) the descriptive name—an idea of what the topic of the list is; 2) the list title; and 3) the subscription address.

Here are some important tips to keep in mind when taking advantage of mailing lists:

✔ *The main address for a mail list will allow you to submit articles, responses, and questions, as well as read the mail posted by other list members. To join a list, do not write to the main address. Instead, enter the subscription address first.*

- You are talking to another computer. Observe and use specific "code" words required in your message area.

- Be specific in your request. There are many lists available, so choose your groups carefully.

- Turn off your signature (the signature is the automatic feature that most e-mail programs allow you to append to your letter including things like your name and e-mail address). If your e-mail program has a "signature" feature, make sure it is turned off to avoid confusing the computer.

- Save the "welcome" message from each list. Upon joining a list, keep the first automatically-generated message; it contains helpful instructions and necessary commands for "unsubscribing" (ending your subscription).

- Once again, subscribe in moderation. Mail lists can easily flood you with too much to read. If you're not careful, just retrieving a day's mail can take 20 minutes—without reading a word of it.

Now you're ready to choose one to join (look for the "E-Mail" icon next to the resources listed in chapter 7). Try one or two that you know will be of interest to you, and then see how much maintenance it takes to be involved. After participating for a week or so, if you find that the information is not what you expected, or becomes to burdensome, simply "unsubscribe" and try another.

GOPHER

**THIS ROADSIGN ICON INDICATES A GOPHER RESOURCE
IN THE "HOMESCHOOL RESOURCE DIRECTORY" IN CHAPTER 7.**

Gopher It!

Gopher was developed at the University of Minnesota in 1991. If you're from that part of the country, you may have guessed that the system is named after the university's mascot. Gopher was designed to offer on-campus Internet users convenient access to internal as well as remote information resources. The "subterranean" information network is referred to as "Gopherspace", with the individual servers sometimes known as "Gopher holes."

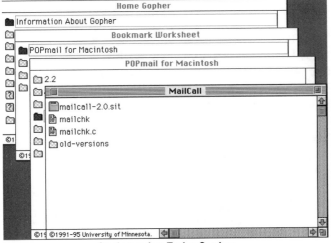

Gopher using Turbo Gopher

Gopher is an information system used to organize and distribute information and resources that are arranged in a hierarchical menu or folder form. Gopher is "text only," so it is not as widely used as the World Wide Web; however, it is a powerful and relatively easy-to-use tool for locating resources on the Internet. Gopher servers are organized geographically by continent, country, state, and university or organization.

✔ *Client-Server is a commonly used buzz-word in many computer publications. It sounds impressive or even intimidating, but in simple terms, the "client" is a program (a piece of software) that enables your computer to retrieve and hold certain types of information (like a Gopher, Web, or FTP file). The "server" is the computer or database that provides the information to the client.*

HOW TO ACCESS GOPHER RESOURCES

Just as the Web began as a text-only information retrieval system, so is Gopher. However, you may now access Gopher resources through graphical browsers, just as you would access Web sites. In fact, many Gopher addresses can be accessed simply by typing in a known Web address, and substituting "gopher://gopher." instead of "http://www."

Gopher is designed for you to browse through the menu hierarchies until you locate the information you need. FTP, or File Transfer Protocol (discussed in a later chapter) requires you to enter an exact destination and directory for the items you are trying to access. With Gopher, however, you do not need to know a specific gopher address you are seeking; you may simply keep exploring folders until you locate a file that looks promising.

If you subscribe to an online service, you most likely have access to Gopher simply by clicking on a button. America Online, for example, has an easy-to-use interface that organizes information into major subject headings such as Education or Religion. If you are using a browser with a direct Internet connection you can enter the URL of the address of the Gopher site you wish to investigate such as "gopher://gopher.site.com" in the URL space of your browser.

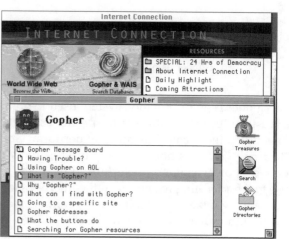

The opening Gopher screen on AOL.

CHAPTER 3· GOPHER IT!

If you are using a text-based client, enter "gopher" at the prompt, then the specific gopher site such as "gopher// gopher.site.com". Or use the program Turbo Gopher, which makes searching Gopherspace an easy task. TurboGopher can be downloaded free of charge from just about any Internet resource forum.

Although much information is still stored in Gopher sites, the World Wide Web is quickly displacing Gopher as the preeminent source for storing and retrieving information. In fact, many older Gopher sites are being rapidly transformed into Web sites. Since most newer Web browsers (such as Mosaic and Netscape, for example) also support Gopher addresses, the two services can be used easily from within one program; however, one Internet vehicle—undoubtedly the World Wide Web—will ultimately become the dominant source for all forms of data and communication.

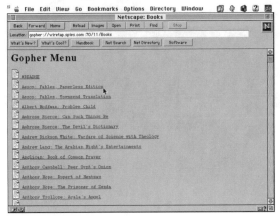

A sample Gopher page in Netscape. Just point and click! Find and download classic books, Christian writings, and Bible translations from this site at: gopher://gopher.wiretap.spies.com.

FTP

**THIS ROADSIGN ICON INDICATES AN FTP RESOURCE
IN THE "HOMESCHOOL RESOURCE DIRECTORY" IN CHAPTER 7.**

CHAPTER 4

To FTP or PPP—That is The Question!

Is it a verb? Is it a phrase? Or is it…a Shakespearean ploy? Oy! The Internet does have its share of intimidating lingo and abbreviations that at first may all sound alike—but be brave! If you hope to harvest the crops of freeware and shareware on the cyberplains, you'll need to know the basics. Fortunately, using FTP is simple if you subscribe to an online service. If you're flying solo on a local ISP, however, then you may have a slightly more complicated set-up; however, your ISP should help you configure your software.

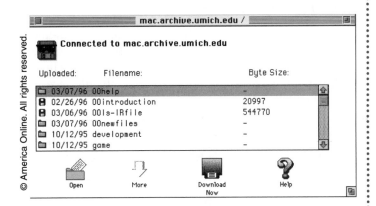

The opening FTP menu on AOL

WHAT IS FTP AND WHY DO I NEED IT?

FTP stands for File Transfer Protocol. This protocol allows a user's program (such as is available with a subscription to a major online service, or with a helper application like Fetch) to transfer files to and from FTP servers. The primary reason most people access FTP

✔ For casual browsing, an online service such as AOL (shown at left) or CompuServe is still the quickest and easiest way to access Internet resources such as FTP sites.

If you want or need to explore these resources in-depth, however, the primary advantage of a local ISP is unlimited "FREE" hours for flat monthly fee (see Chapter 1 for details).

✔ *When you are downloading application programs over the Internet, particularly from anonymous FTP sites, there is always a risk that the files may be infected with a computer virus which can corrupt or destroy other files stored on your computer. We recommend that you either purchase a good virus protection program, or download a freeware version (visit the "comp.virus" newsgroup for more information. You cannot catch a virus from data files (text, graphics, etc.—just software programs like games or utilities. "Secure" online services like AOL or CompuServe check uploaded files, so viruses are very rare from these sources.*

sites is for free software. Other common uses include storage of documents and graphics for Web pages (uploaded by the creators) or the transfer of large files by commercial users such as publishers and printers.

WHAT IS "ANONYMOUS" FTP?

Many businesses and organizations store secure data in private FTP sites for retrieval by authorized users with passcodes. You will likely never see these sites, since they are not "browsable" like the World Wide Web. Public FTP sites, on the other hand, are labeled "anonymous" because the files available there come from many different unnamed sources. In addition, the computers these files are stored on do not care who you are—anyone that can access an FTP server can download FTP files free of charge. To do this, simply use "anonymous" as your username and your Internet e-mail address as your password.

HOW TO USE FTP RESOURCES

Whether you access FTP sites through an online service, or via your local or national Internet service provider, chances are you will be using a graphical client (software program) as opposed to a text-only interface. A

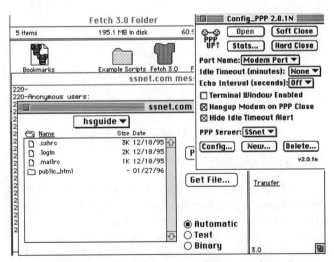

A FTP menu with Fetch, and the PPP control panel

program called Fetch is the most popular FTP tool for the Macintosh, while WinSock FTP is the mainstay for Windows machines. Whichever platform you are on, you simply need to switch on your modem, and launch the FTP application or online program.

Each FTP resource has an address, which includes the name of the computer or organization at which the information is stored. Type this address into your FTP program's address field. This will take you to the location of the information you want. From there, you will need to follow the path listed beneath most addresses. A path is a list of directory (or folder) names separated by slashes. Find the directory named first, then locate the next folder name in the path, and so on, until you get to the actual file name you are looking for.

The "Homeschool Resource Directory" in Chapter 7 includes many FTP sites for you to explore. During your travels, you will likely encounter different types of data files, indicated by assorted types of file extensions (the suffix of the file name, after the last period). Here are a few common file extensions, or suffixes, along with the types of files they delineate:

✔ *Freeware is software that you can use forever without any requirement for remuneration by the author.*

Shareware, on the other hand, may be "tried out" for free, but if you continue to use it, must be registered with the author (usually for a nominal fee) in order to qualify for support, updates, extended capabilities, documentation, etc.

It's a great free enterprise system, so support it by remitting the fee for shareware you decide to keep and use—otherwise, delete it from your hard drive.

.txt   A common text file—usually in ASCII format (can be read by all computers).

.gif   Graphic Interchange Format—a picture file which can be read by most programs.

.jpg   Short for JPEG—Joint Photographic Experts Group, a standard format for compressed graphic images

.mpg
.avi
.mov   These three extensions all indicate different standards for motion video (MPEG is the most common).

.zip   PC compressed files—Can be uncompressed with PKUnzip (downloadable).

CHAPTER 4 · TO FTP OR PPP—THAT IS THE QUESTION!

USENET

**THIS ROADSIGN ICON INDICATES A USENET RESOURCE
IN THE "HOMESCHOOL RESOURCE DIRECTORY" IN CHAPTER 7.**

CHAPTER 5

Perusing USENET

USENET is an Internet messaging system which allows special interest groups (known as newsgroups) to communicate in a manner similar to e-mail.

Each newsgroup is like a big bulletin board with its own purpose. Anyone with access to the Internet can **post** to newsgroups, or respond to anything posted to any newsgroup. Subscribing, or joining, a newsgroup allows you to post your thoughts and ideas much like you would in an online forum.

There are a few extra rules to abide by when posting messages to USENET. Read the FAQ (frequently asked questions) before asking questions about the group. Read the thread (the group of messages on a specific topic) before posting your own message style. Be sure to stay within a given thread when posting. USENET newsgroup is not the place for sending personal responses to other posters. Send them e-mail if your message is only meant for them. Following these simple guidelines will keep you from getting flamed (insulted or reprimanded) by old-timers.

✔ *Most newsreaders keep a hotlist of your newsgroup subscriptions for easy access.*

✔ *Newsgroup messages (known as articles) are delivered via the UNIX-based network called USENET. Both UNIX and non-UNIX computers can participate in USENET because of how the system uses forwarding to collect and distribute the items to the appropriate sites.*

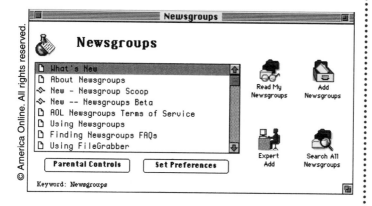

USENET newsgroup names consist of several words, each separated by a period. The first word is the hierarchy which tells you what type of group you are looking at (i.e., comp. or misc.). The second and third words describe the subject of the newsgroup.

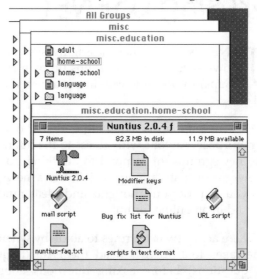

Viewing newsgroups with one of many available newsreaders

There are thousands of USENET servers around the world that host the same group of forums, and therefore share messages as they are posted. Messages generally appear within twelve hours.

There are two types of hierarchies—mainstream and alternative. Some mainstream hierarchies are:

- comp—computer related

- misc—miscellaneous groups

- news—news about the Internet

- rec—recreation: sports, hobbies, games

- sci—science related

- soc—social issues

- talk—the Internet version of talk radio.

Some alternative hierarchies are:

- alt—alternative groups

- bionet—biology

- bitnet—bitnet related

- biz—business related

- info—information on the Internet

- k12—school related.

If you cannot find a specific newsgroup that covers the subject you are looking for you can even suggest that your specific interest be formed into a new newsgroup. However, considering that there are nearly 3000 different newsgroups currently available, you will probably find more than enough to keep you busy reading and posting.

Be sure to browse through the Homeschool Resource Directory (chapter 7) for a large selection of different Newsgroups to investigate.

WWW

THIS ROADSIGN ICON INDICATES A WEB RESOURCE
IN THE "HOMESCHOOL RESOURCE DIRECTORY" IN CHAPTER 7.

CHAPTER 6

Traffic's Not Crawling on the Web

The World Wide Web is the newest and fastest onramp to the information superhighway. Its user friendly, graphical user interface (GUI) is paving the way for millions of new netizens. This interface includes graphics, sound, video clips, 3-D worlds, and much more.

✔ *The backbone of the Web is called HTTP (HyperText Transport Protocol); that is why each Web address begins with "http://".*

WHAT IS THE WORLD WIDE WEB?

The World Wide Web was developed at CERN (the European Laboratory for Particle Physics) in Switzerland in 1990. Although the terms Web and Internet are often used synonymously, the Web is actually a fairly modern means of *conveyance* with which to navigate and view locations on the Net. Originally a text-based medium for standardizing reports and data from around the world, the Web has been transformed into a graphical interface, and is quickly becoming a tool for delivering multimedia content (sound, animation, and eventually video) across the Internet.

To gain access to the Web, you need a browser program such as Netscape, Mosaic, or Microsoft's new Internet Explorer, which is built into the latest Windows operating system. Some online services such as America Online and Prodigy also provide built-in browsers. The browser program is stored like any other application on your hard drive. It reads and displays information and graphics based on HTML (Hypertext Markup Language), the standardized page-description language of the World Wide Web.

A Web page nearly always contains links to other pages or resources. These links are based on an address-

✔ *Download your choice of Web browsers for free! Mosaic is available from "ftp.ncsa .uiuc.edu" in the /Mosaic/Windows or /Mosaic/Mac directories.*

Netscape is available free from "http://www. netscape.com."

Be sure to follow instructions in the "README" files included in the download.

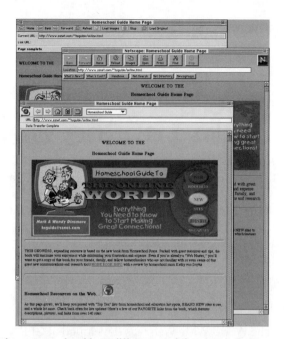

Here's an example of how different each browser's features can be. Each banner has different buttons for various features, and each browser displays the images and text uniquely. Browsers shown here: AOL, Netscape and Mosaic.

ing system called URL. In this unique way whole groups of information are joined into one graphical document that invites you to follow links by clicking on highlighted text or graphics.

You can gain access to the Web either by subscribing to a major online service that includes Web access (and often their own browser), or by a SLIP/PPP direct connection (see chapter 1) to the Internet via an ISP, using one of the many web browsers on the market.

Once connected to the Web, you can interact easily with people around the world. No longer the sole realm of "nerds," "hackers," and "techies," today's Internet access through the Web is a refreshing, unintimidating experience. How can I create my own Web page?

BONUS SECTION: BUILD YOUR OWN WEB PAGE!

Designing and publishing your own World Wide Web Home Page is really simpler than it sounds... and it's getting easier every day. Many homeschool families already have their own home page. They vary from a simple collection of links and family interests, to full scale productions with regular newsletters and support group meetings via Internet chat (like a Newsgroup discussion only live). Thanks to a growing number of new software programs, together with "built-in" host computer server space provided by your Internet or online service provider, you can put a simple page on the Internet in as little as one afternoon or evening. More complicated Web sites, of course, require much more practice and patience, along with a willingness to experiment (try, try again), and follow good writing and design principles.

Don't be afraid, however, that you have to get it right the first time. One of the greatest benefits of publishing on the World Wide Web is that you can change it any time you like. Correcting a mistake or making an improvement only takes a few minutes—so you'll have plenty of opportunity to polish your work. The important thing to begin is: just do it!

STEP ONE: Deciding What to Publish

This first requirement seems pretty obvious, but you'd be surprised at the number of Web pages that appear to have been constructed without more than, "Look, Mom, my picture is on the World Wide Web." If you've done any amount of surfing at all, you may already have an idea for creating a page with a unique theme. If not, that's ok too. There's nothing wrong with creating a "me too" page your first time out. The process is a little like writing your first poem, or giving your first speech; you're a little unsure of what one is supposed to be in the first place, and you certainly don't know all of the rules of style, form, and etiquette. Fortunately, as we'll show you later, there are new tools to help you overcome any initial stage fright you may have.

✔ *Those who are more programming-oriented may prefer writing their HTML code from scratch. Such folk may obtain "A Beginner's Guide to HTML" at: http://www.ncsa.ui uc.edu/General/Inte rnet/WWW/HTML Primer.html*

STEP TWO: Organize Your Thoughts

So, let's choose a subject! How about creating a Web page on: your favorite pet or zoo animal, your family's latest unit study, a recent field trip, your home town's history and geography, a how-to guide for a certain craft or hobby project, or a biographical page on a favorite role model or historical character?

Once you have a concept, it helps to begin with an outline—particularly since making a Web page has so much in common with other creative writing endeavors. Begin with some original material from your own experience, then search for links to sites that enhance or support your own perspective. From your outline, determine if the content can fit on one page, or if each major point should have a page of its own. It's not critical to set your site up this way to start with, but it's nice to know that you can expand as your content—and links to related content—grow.

STEP THREE: Creating the HTML Document

Although you can sit down to learn how to write in raw HTML (12 months ago this was the only option), we recommend either an HTML editor or WYSIWYG Web authoring program such as GNN Press (By NaviSoft, an AOL division) or Adobe PageMill. Each of these packages costs about $100, but we have found them extremely helpful in building and launching our own Web sites.

Each of these packages will allow you to import or paste text from your word processing files, as well as establish anchors and links. Of course, you can also enter text directly in the program. You can also experiment with graphics, colors, and patterns. GNN Press (formerly NaviPress) comes with a large library of clip-art and graphic enhancements, such as rules and bullets, to decorate and personalize your page. PageMill does not have such a collection, but provides other advanced features such as raw HTML support, easier image map creation, and the ability to create forms.

STEP FOUR: Uploading and Storing Your Page

Many online services and ISP's allow you 1 or 2 MB of server storage as part of your monthly service package. Most homemade home pages will never need more than this amount, but if you decide to publish your entire family history, with pictures of every member (and their pets) since the invention of photography, then you will likely need to pay for additional server space.

The trickiest part, really, of becoming a Web author is understanding how to transfer files by FTP from your computer to your service provider's Web server. If you are on an online service, such as AOL, then there is an easy interface for uploading your files to the Web in their Internet connection area. If you are online through an ISP you'll want to download a very handy program called Fetch. This will make uploading your files a snap.

STEP FIVE: If You Build It, They MIGHT Come

Putting a message on your new home page and expecting it to be read by millions is comparable to wearing a t-shirt in a crowded New York subway and expecting everyone to see the imprinted message. To get the exposure you want, you'll need to publicize and promote your site. There are a number of ways to do this for free. 1) You can send e-mail to other homeschool sites and ask to "trade links" with each other. 2) You can also submit your URL (personal Web address) to several popular search engines so that when people search for sites containing homeschool or homeschooling, yours may turn up in the list. A search engine is a service provided on the Web for locating specific URLs. You simply enter the topic, such as homeschooling, in the space provided and a list will be returned. There will usually be a "submit your URL" button at the top of the Web page, click on this button and follow their directions to add your home page to their directory. 3) Best of all, visit Homeschool Guide's Web site and send us a note. We love to see new pages and regularly review pages nominated for HSG's "Top 5% of Homeschool Websites."

✔ *A "Home Page" may be complete in itself, but is more often simply the first page in a multi-page "Web Site." The home page is actually comparable to a book cover or the table of contents. Subsequent pages are like chapter heads, which contain both content and links to other sites of similar interest.*

RESOURCES

250 I-Sites

WE HOPE YOU ENJOY YOUR TRAVELS ON THE
INTERNET! DON'T FORGET TO "BUCKLE UP!"

Homeschool Resource Directory

Homeschooling

ABBA MINISTRIES

Homeschooling and Christian Resources

http://members.gnn.com/cgonz/gospel.htm

✽✽✽

✔ *The little icon signs tell you which type of Internet protocol you're looking up, so you can use the correct software to access each resource.*

ABOUT HOME SCHOOLING IN MONTGOMERY COUNTY

gopher://gopher.mciu.k12.pa.us:70/00/resourcecenter/instructionalcouncil/homeschool/abouthomeschool

✽✽✽

ADVICE TO NEW HOME SCHOOLERS

Here is some advice gleaned from other homeschoolers. Once you've made the decision to home school and begin the comittment, there's no better place to go for advice than these seasoned homeschoolers.

http://www.ici.net/cust_pages/taadah/advise.html

✽✽✽

AMERICAN HOMESCHOOL PUBLISHING

American Homeschool Publishing provides outstanding educational resources and products from over 40 publishers at discounted prices.

http://www.doubled.com/ahsp/

✻✻✻

AUSTRALIAN HOME SCHOOLERS RESOURCE PAGE

This page has been set up for Australian homeschoolers (and anyone else interested) to provide information, support contacts and a starting place for homeschoolers embarking on journeys across the Internet.

http://brisbane.DIALix.oz.au/~threedp/homeschool

✻✻✻

BACKYARD SCIENTIST

A great homeschool science resource page to visit with science and fun from the Backyard Scientist. Jane Hoffman, the Backyard Scientist, is an author and a sought-after speaker at public education and homeschooling conferences.

http://www.cts.com/~netsales/herc/bysexp.htm

✻✻✻

B.E.A.C.H.

Beach Educators Association for Creative Homeschooling.

http://wwwp.exis.net/~dplast/beach.htm

✻✻✻

BIBLICAL FOUNDATIONS FOR CHRISTIAN HOMESCHOOLING

In response to God's Word in Deuteronomy 6:5-7. Very helpful pages filled with wonderful resources for homeschool families.

http://pages.prodigy.com/MA/christianhmsc/

✳✳✳

CHOOSING CURRICULUM

" Sometimes one of the most difficult things to do when we're homeschooling is to CHOOSE CURRICULUM!" And more helpful information by Tamara Eaton

http://199.227.115.30/homeschool/tips-3.htm

✳✳✳

CHRISTIAN HOMESCHOOLERS HOMEPAGE

A Christian family's homeschool home page.

http://www.docker.com/~reedyd/homescho.html

✳✳✳

CHRISTIAN HOMESCHOOLING HOMEPAGES

Homepages and documents containing valuable information and resources.

http://pages.prodigy.com/MA/christianhmsc/christianhm-sc.html

✳✳✳

CHRISTIAN HOMESCHOOL NEWSGROUP

A moderated newsgroup for Christians to share and compare along their homeschool journey.

alt.education.home-school.christian

✳✳✳

THE CHRISTIAN INTERACTIVE NETWORK'S CHRISTIAN HOMESCHOOL FORUM PAGE

A wonderful homeschoolers support system on the Web sponsored by the Christian Interactive Network. With topics including: getting started, favorite HS tips, book reviews, and a lot more to enrich homeschoolers.

URL: http://www.gocin.com/homeschool/

✳✳✳

CHRISTIAN RESOURCE DATABASE

Homeschooling, literature, Bible studies, Bibles, online, childrens ministries, Christian homepages, Christian resource lists, clip art, college and university, electronic magazines, frequently asked questions, humor, Internet search engine and more.

http://www.cforc.com/christian.cgi

✳✳✳

COLONIAL SCHOOL DISTRICT HOME SCHOOLING POLICY

gopher://gopher.mciu.k12.pa.us:70/00/resourcecenter/instructionalcouncil/homeschool/districtpolicy/colonial

CLONLARA SCHOOL HOME BASED EDUCATION PROGRAM NEWS

Clonlara School Home Based Education Program News: Over 2000 families are enrolled in Clonlara School's Home Based Education Program. Their new computer-based education program is up and running with seven courses online and several students already enrolled.

http://www.grfn.org/education/clonlara/index17.html

✳✳✳

 ESSAYS ON HOMESCHOOLING

Jim Muncy says, "Here are some of my thoughts on various aspects of homeschooling. Most of these originated as posts to one of the homeschooling lists."

http://www.valdosta.peachnet.edu/~muncyj/homeschooling/thoughts.html

✳✳✳

FAMILY MATTERS: WHY HOMESCHOOLING MAKES SENSE

By David Guterson, a public-school teacher and a homeschooling parent. Filled with much wisdom.

http://www2.portal.ca/~comprev/proglib/guterson.htm

✳✳✳

FOCUSING ON FAMILIES: STRATEGIES FOR IMPROVING HOME-SCHOOL RELATIONSHIPS

gopher://gopher.nwrel.org:70/00/news/newsletters/equityinfo/v2n1_dec94/parent.txt

CHAPTER 7 · HOMESCHOOL RESOURCE DIRECTORY

GREENLEAF PRESS HOME PAGE

Here's where you can find out about Greenleaf Press products (especially the History Study Packages) order packages and supplemental books, find out about Rob and Cyndy Shearer's speaking schedule, and much more.

http://www.gocin.com/Greenleaf/top.htm

✳✳✳

GROWING WITHOUT SCHOOLING

Susannah Sheffer says "Homeschooling refers to the concept of letting kids learn at home and in the surrounding community, rather than in school. What kinds of people homeschool? All kinds."

http://www2.portal.ca/~comprev/proglib/holt.htm

✳✳✳

HIGHSCHOOLER'S HOMESCHOOLING PAGE

The place to go for "expert" advice—directly from a high school homeschool student.

http://www.cis.upenn.edu/~brada/hsquestions.html

✳✳✳

HOME EDUCATORS' RESOURCES ONLINE

Brought to you by Ronald J. Bowden—Your Resource Center for Home Education Information.

http://www.win.net/~heart_talk/hero.html

✳✳✳

HOME-ED-KIDS!

Information and resources for "home-ed" kids and families. Many useful features.

http://sara.zia.com/

✻✻✻

HOME-ED WEB SURFING PAGE

Resource pointer for "surfing" the Web.

http://www.charm.net/~jcain/surfin.html

✻✻✻

HOMEFRONT/HOMESCHOOLING

This page contains good homeschooling and general education links.

http://funnelweb.utcc.utk.edu/~recon77/educ.html

✻✻✻

HOME LEARNING SOFTWARE

Educational fun for the whole family. A catalog with disks that teach Bible, math, science, art, language arts, history, geography, languages, computer, music, preschool skills, and more.

http://members.aol.com/homelearn/

✻✻✻

HOME EDUCATION RADIO NETWORK

HEN Radio is a live, call-in radio program addressing the needs of homeschool families. Hosted by homeschooling mom Vicki Brady HEN Radio airs every Saturday, 1pm to 3pm eastern.

http://www.ici.net/cust_pages/taadah/hen.html

✳✳✳

HOMESCHOOL INFORMATION

Information on the various homeschool organizations, FAQ's on homeschooling, and FAQ's on computers.

http://www.halcyon.com/jerome/homesch.html

✳✳✳

HOMESCHOOLING SOURCES

This site contains information on taking responsibility for your children's education at home rather than schooling them outside the home. Includes print media, books, magazines, and growing without schooling.

http://www.cais.com/aevans/homestead/homesch.html

✳✳✳

HOMESCHOOLING CHILDREN WITH SPECIAL NEEDS

For children with special needs, such as those with physical, psychological, or learning disabilities (ADD, ADHD, dyslexia, etc.).

http://www.ici.net/cust_pages/taadah/spnd.html

✳✳✳

HOMESCHOOLING FOR UNSCHOOLERS

A home page with helpful resources for those who believe along the lines of Mark Twain: "I have never let my schooling interfere with my education." Great educational links!

http://www.islandnet.com/~bedford/home_lrn.html

✳✳✳

HOMESCHOOL NEWSGROUP CHRISTIAN

An unmoderated newsgroup for Christians to discuss any and all aspects of homeschooling.

misc.education.home-school.christian

✳✳✳

HOMESCHOOL NEWSGROUP

An unmoderated secular newsgroup for the discussion of homeschooling issues.

misc.education.home-school.misc

✳✳✳

HOMESCHOOLING

Hot homework topics, Freenet's schoolhouse, distance learning , and more educational resources.

gopher://dpl20.denver.lib.co.us:70/11/Learning%20Reso
urces%20and%20Homework%20

✳✳✳

CHAPTER 7 · HOMESCHOOL RESOURCE DIRECTORY

HOMESCHOOLING INFO GUIDES

gopher://ericir.syr.edu:70/00/InfoGuides/Fall_1994/Hom eSchooling3

✻✻✻

HOMESCHOOL GOPHER

Contains FAQs, announcements, and other homeschool resources information.

gopher://lib.NMSU.edu:70/11/.subjects/Education/Home schooling

✻✻✻

HOMESCHOOL INTERNET RESOURCES

A gopher of electronic journals and newsletters for home-schoolers.

gopher://ericir.syr.edu/00/InfoGuides/Fall_1994/HomeSc hooling2

✻✻✻

HOME-ED-POLITICS-@MAINSTREAM.COM

This list discusses legal issues around homeschooling.

Address:

home-ed-politics-request@mainstream.com

subscribe home-ed-politics first name & last name

✻✻✻

HMEDRSCH@ETSUADMN.ETSU.EDU

The Home Education Research Discussion List.

A moderated list for people researching the subject of home education.

Address:

hmedrsch-request@etsuadmn.etsu.edu

Describe your interest and activities in home schooling research.

✳✳✳

HOME-ED@WORLD.STD.COM

A broader home education list.

Address:

home-ed-request@world.std.com

✳✳✳

HOMESCHOOL RESOURCES

gopher://nysernet.org:70/0R7428-8787-
/ftp%20archives/listserv/publib/1993/Apr/930412

✳✳✳

HOMESCHOOLING

gopher://SJUVM.STJOHNS.EDU:2070/00/listserv/list$n
b/edstyle/94%2507%2507%2021:24%20%20%2058%2
0%20%20Re:%20Home%20Schooling

✳✳✳

HOMESCHOOLING AND STYLES

gopher://SJUVM.STJOHNS.EDU:2070/00/listserv/list$
nb/edstyle/93%2505%2517%2006:04%20%20%2055%
20%20%20Re:%20Styles%20and%20Home%20School
ing

✻✻✻

HOMESCHOOL CENTERS

gopher://nysernet.org:70/0R6035-6882-
/ftp%20archives/listserv/publib/1993/Apr/930409

✻✻✻

HOMESCHOOLING INFORMATION REQUESTED

gopher://nysernet.org:70/0R3048-4441-
/ftp%20archives/listserv/pubyac/941031

✻✻✻

HOMESCHOOLING

gopher://nysernet.org:70/0R2291-3237-
/ftp%20archives/listserv/publib/1994/940803

✻✻✻

HOMESCHOOLING

gopher://nysernet.org:70/0R2291-3237-
/Special%20Collections:%20Libraries/Publib%20Archive
/1994/940803

✻✻✻

HOMESCHOOLERS IN YOUR LIBRARY

gopher://nysernet.org:70/0R11715-13025-
/ftp%20archives/listserv/pubyac/940926

✳✳✳

HOMESCHOOLING INFO GUIDES

gopher://inform.umd.edu:7070/0gopher://ericir.syr.edu:7
0/00/InfoGuides/Fall_1994/HomeSchooling4

✳✳✳

HOMESCHOOLING FAQ

gopher://inform.umd.edu:7070/0gopher://ericir.syr.edu:7
0/00/FAQ/Homeschooling

✳✳✳

HOMESCHOOLING

gopher://gopher.mciu.k12.pa.us:70/11/resourcecenter/in
structionalcouncil/homeschool

✳✳✳

HOMESCHOOLING IN WEST VIRGINIA

gopher://gopher.mciu.k12.pa.us:70/00/resourcecenter/in
structionalcouncil/homeschool/risehomeschool/wvhome-
schlabstract

✳✳✳

CHAPTER 7 · HOMESCHOOL RESOURCE DIRECTORY

HOMESCHOOLING IN WEST VIRGINIA BY LEE STOUGH

gopher://gopher.mciu.k12.pa.us:70/00/resourcecenter/instructionalcouncil/homeschool/risehomeschool/wvhome-schl.excerpt

✳✳✳

HOMESCHOOLING AND THE LAW, BY MARTHA MCCARTHY

gopher://gopher.mciu.k12.pa.us:70/00/resourcecenter/instructionalcouncil/homeschool/risehomeschool/home-schllawabstract

✳✳✳

HOMESCHOOL LIBRARIES

gopher://garnet.msen.com:70/0R77971-79990-1m/vendor/maven/mlist/old/METRONET.LOG9404

✳✳✳

HOMESCHOOLING LIBRARIES

gopher://garnet.msen.com:70/0R520968-522987-1m/vendor/maven/mlist/old/met.1994

✳✳✳

HOMESCHOOLING GUIDES

gopher://ericir.syr.edu:70/00/InfoGuides/Fall_1994/HomeSchooling4

HOMESCHOOLING ARCHIVES

gopher://riceinfo.rice.edu:1170/0R279178-283904-
/More/Watch/archivesep94

✳✳✳

HOMESCHOOL INTERACTIVE

gopher://riceinfo.rice.edu:1170/0R236552-238299-
/More/Watch/archivemar94

✳✳✳

HOMESCHOOLERS AND REFERENCE SERVICE

gopher://burrow.cl.msu.edu:70/0R48296-51958-
/news/archives/bit.listserv.libref-l/bll.9410

✳✳✳

HOMESCHOOL CONNECTION

gopher://burrow.cl.msu.edu:70/00/msu/dept/educ/grad/9
4-95assist/research/college/dchome

✳✳✳

HOMESCHOOLING LITTLE ONES

Excellent tips by Tamara Eaton of CIN.

http://199.227.115.30/homeschool/Tips-5.htm

✳✳✳

HOMESCHOOLING- A CHOICE TO EDUCATE AT HOME

More and more parents are pulling their children out of public schools and teaching their children the knowledge and values they want them to learn. Home schooling seems to be the answer to some families but is it as simple as it seems?

http://www.impactol.org/iol/education/homesch.html

✳✳✳

HOMESCHOOLING

A page of lists of homeschool and educational links.

http://www.contra.org/~mwatts/homeschool/

✳✳✳

HOMESCHOOLING INFORMATION CENTER ANNEX

This annex is a recent front page (with some of the material non-members cannot access removed) from the Prodigy "Homeschooling Information Center."

http://pages.prodigy.com/K/I/S/kids/hmsc.htm

✳✳✳

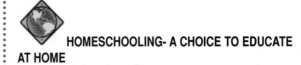

HOMESCHOOLING SOURCES

This page contains information on taking responsibility for your children's education at home.

http://www.cais.com/aevans/homestead/homesch.html

✳✳✳

HOMESCHOOLING CANADA

Home schooling programs allow students to complete their education from grades 1 through 12 at home. The School Act recognizes that education in Alberta can be delivered to students in a variety of ways. This page will help you with that information.

http://ednet.edc.gov.ab.ca/level3/adlc/400/homeed.html

✳✳✳

HOMESCHOOL NETWORK PAGE

http://indy.inre.asu.edu/~sam/vanraap.html

✳✳✳

JOHNSON HOMESCHOOL'S HOME PAGE

About the Johnson's Homeschooled children. Stephen, Heather, Kathi, Kirke, and Stephen. The best place to learn all you need to know about homeschooling is from other home-schooling families!

http://www.stonehenge.com/~jhs/

✳✳✳

KIDS@HOME MAGAZINE

The Magazine written by and for homeschoolers.

http://www.transport.com/~kidshome/kah.html

✳✳✳

CHAPTER 7 · HOMESCHOOL RESOURCE DIRECTORY

LOVING EDUCATION AT HOME (LEAH)

"Loving Education At Home is a Christian organization, the members of which are likeminded Christian home education support groups made up of families dedicated to observing the Biblical commands of Deuteronomy 6:4-10, Proverbs 22:6, and Ephesians 6:4. We promote home education as the Scriptural."

http://www.servtech.com/public/dls/hs/leah/index.html

✳✳✳

MANITOBA HOMESCHOOL RESOURCE PAGE

Here is an opportunity for homeschoolers everywhere to share information, friendship, and even projects. Have you ever wondered why people, especially Canadians, homeschool? Are you curious about reasons for considering homeschool as an alternative to public or private schools? Then visit the Manitoba Homeschool Resource Page.

http://www.mts.net/~jcampbel/index.html

✳✳✳

MOM'S AT HOME PAGE

This site is especially for (but certainly not limited to) those moms who are foregoing full-time paid employment to raise their children. It is also for those considering it! Dads-at-Home are welcome too!

http://iquest.com/~jsm/moms/index.html

✳✳✳

CHAPTER 7 · HOMESCHOOL RESOURCE DIRECTORY

NEW ATTITUDE (CUTTING EDGE CHRISTIAN COUNTER CULTURE) BY JOSH HARRIS

The mission of New Attitude is to challenge teens to reach their full potential for Jesus Christ. Joshua Harris founded New Attitude at the age of seventeen with a dream to link together fellow Christian home schoolers.

In a world full of public school peers, it's easy to feel alone. New Attitude has helped to change that by providing a forum and outlet for the creative energy of the first generation of home-school teens.

URL: http://www.newattitude.com/~joshuah/

✳✳✳

OREGON HOME SCHOOLING

gopher://gopher.state.or.us:70/1D-1:21873:g%20Home%20Schooling

✳✳✳

PARENTS ARE TEACHERS HOME PAGE

This area is for those who are currently involved in home-schooling or want to become more involved in their child's education. Information available on homeschooling resources.

http://yn.la.ca.us/academy_one/teacher/menu.pat.html

✳✳✳

CHAPTER 7 · HOMESCHOOL RESOURCE DIRECTORY

POTTSTOWN SCHOOL DISTRICT
HOME SCHOOLING POLICY

gopher://gopher.mciu.k12.pa.us:70/00/resourcecenter/instructionalcouncil/homeschool/districtpolicy/pottstown

✳✳✳

PRACTICAL HOMESCHOOLING AND
HOMESCHOOLING PC ON "HOME SCHOOL WORLD"

Bill and Mary Pride's Web site. Many unique and valuable resources. Sections include: Practical Homeschooling with articles from back issues, Homeschool PC, Homeschool People and Places (pages for all major state and national homeschool groups, with event calendars, laws for every state, membership info, and more) and the Homeschool Mall (ads and demos for dozens of homeschool products).

http://www.home-school.com

✳✳✳

RESOURCES FOR HOMESCHOOLERS

"Reading, Rhythm and Rom" –several pointers to good homeschool links.

http://www.wco.com/~readrom/home.html

✳✳✳

RISE BIBLIOGRAPHY ON HOMESCHOOLING

gopher://gopher.mciu.k12.pa.us:70/00/resourcecenter/instructionalcouncil/homeschool/risehomeschool/risebibliohomeschool

✳✳✳

SERVING HOMESCHOOLERS

gopher://nysernet.org:70/0R2807-3938-/ftp%20archives/listserv/publib/1994/940926

✳✳✳

SYCAMORE TREE HOMESCHOOL CATALOG

Sycamore Tree, Inc., providing homeschool educational services to students in grades K-12 all over the world, is a catalog purchasing service with more than 3000 educational items.

http://www.sycamoretree.com/home.html

✳✳✳

"TAFFIE"

Taffie is a mailing list for home schoolers in Texas.

Address:

listproc@jsoft.com
with "subscribe taffie" & your name in the body of the message.

✳✳✳

CHAPTER 7 · HOMESCHOOL RESOURCE DIRECTORY

TAKING CHILDREN SERIOUSLY

This list, sponsored by Sarah Lawrence of the British home-schooling magazine, is not strictly a homeschooling mailing list. It is devoted to serious discussion of what it means to raise children as human beings in their own right.

Subscribe TCS-list (your e-mail address) to listserv@netcom.com.

✳✳✳

T.E.A. MEETS WITH HOMESCHOOLERS

gopher://gopher.metronet.com:70/00/North-Texas-Free-Net/Education-Center/taffie/TM.9

✳✳✳

THE CHRISTIAN HOME EDUCATION PAGE

A family home page with an educational philosophy along the lines of Charlotte Mason with a strong biblical world view and a providential view of history.

http://jps.ns.net/~daa/index.htm

✳✳✳

THE HOMESCHOOL SUPPORT NETWORK'S WEBPAGE!

The Homeschool Support Network (HSN) is a nonprofit service organization working to encourage and equip parents who have chosen to educate their own children. HSN provides information and services to home educating families through their publication Home Educator's Family Times.

http://www.gocin.com/homeschool/support/

CHAPTER 7 · HOMESCHOOL RESOURCE DIRECTORY

THE INTERNET HITS HOME

"Homeschooling Gets a Boost from the Internet"-
Information on the "how and why" of homeschooling.

http://gnn.com/gnn/meta/edu/features/archive/home.html

THE HOMESCHOOL RESOURCE CENTER

Many great resources and services on this page!

http://www.primenet.com/~elvis/home.html

✳✳✳

THE HOMESCHOOL USERS GROUP- MACINTOSH

HUG MAC is a group of individuals who have banded
together to trade ideas about how to get the most out of their
Macs in their home education efforts.

http://members.aol.com/hugmac/hugmac.html

✳✳✳

THE HOMESCHOOLING HOME PAGE

By a homeschooling high school student who started in the
middle of tenth grade because he felt he couldn't put up with
school for another second!

http://www.cis.upenn.edu/~brada/homeschooling.html

✳✳✳

THE HOMESCHOOL PAGE

Provided by the Internet Alaska family, with many useful resources.

http://www.alaska.net:80/~mteel/homesch/homeschl.html

✳✳✳

TRAIN-UP-A-CHILD

A fairly new list to promote and encourage Christian Homeschoolers and Christian Parenting.

Hub@XC.Org

with the message:

subscribe TRAIN-UP-A-CHILD

✳✳✳

TROPICAL HOME SCHOOLER

A newsletter for Island home educators.

http://nko.mhpcc.edu/tdp/ths.html

✳✳✳

UNSCHOOLING

A smaller list with an emphasis on unschooling.

Address:

learning@sea.east.sun.com

Subscription Address:

learning-request@sea.east.sun.com

✳✳✳

UNSCHOOLERS MAILING LIST

A new mailing list for unschoolers.

majordomo@nilenet.com

with the message:

subscribe unschooling-list

Send submissions to:

unschooling-list@nilenet.com

✳✳✳

WAYOUT'S HOMESCHOOL PAGE

A colorful and helpful home page with links and resource information important to homeschoolers.

http://www.localnet.com/~wayout/netscape.html

✳✳✳

Computing

ACADEMC SOFTWARE DEVELOPMENT

A mailing list for the discussion of all aspects of academic and educational software.

Address:

acsoft-l@wuvmd.wustl.edu

Subscription Address:

listserv@wuvmd.wustl.edu

＊＊＊

APPLE

Anonymous FTP:

Address:

ftp.support.apple.com/

＊＊＊

AV MAC SOFWARE AND INFORMATION

Anonymous FTP:

Address:

ftp.csua.berkeley.edu

Path:

/pub/jwang/

＊＊＊

BUSINESS

For the discussion of business computing.

k12.ed.business

***

COMPUTER NETWORKING

A mailing list for discussing the use of computer networking in education.

Address: cneduc-l@tamvm1.tamu.edu

Subscription Address:

listserv@tamvm1.tamu.edu

CHRISTIAN MACINTOSH USERS GROUP

http://www.industrial-artworks.com/cmug/index.html

***

CHILDREN'S SHAREWARE PAGES

http://www.sylvan.com/

***

COMPUTING

For the discussion of curricular computing.

k12.ed.comp.literacy

***

CREATING ALTERNATIVE HIERCHY NEWSGROUPS

FAQ's and guidelines for creating "alt" newsgroups.

Anonymous FTP:

Address:

rtfm.mit.edu

Path:

/pub/usenet/news.answers/alt-config-guide

***

E-ZINE LIST

A list of electronic magazines available on the Internet.

Anonymous FTP:

Address:

etext.archive.umich.edu

Path:

/pub/zines/e-zine-list.gz

***

FREQUENTLY ASKED QUESTIONS (FAQ) MASTER LIST

A master list of all the FAQs available on the Internet.

Anonymous FTP:

Address:

rtfm.mit.edu

Path:

/pub/usenet/news.answers/index

FTP ARCHIVES

Below are several FTP locations to search for freeware and shareware on the Internet. Anonymous FTP sites only allow so many logins at a time, so if one is full try another.

Anonymous FTP:

Address:

ocf.berkeley.edu

Address:

wuarchive.wustl.edu

Address:

sunset.cse.nau.edu

Address:

ftp.uu.net

Address:

rtfm.mit.edu

✳✳✳

HOME PAGE AUTHORING

Tools and tips for creating your own home page.

Anonymous FTP:

Address:

ftp.netcom.com

Path:

/pub/iceman/VC/hpa.html

✳✳✳

LISTS OF USENET NEWSGROUPS

Anonymous FTP:

Address:

rtfm.mit.edu

Paths:

/pub/usenet/news.answers/active-newsgroups/part 1

/pub/usenet/news.answers/active-newsgroups/part 2

✳✳✳

MACINTOSH ARCHIVES

Anonymous FTP:

Address:

oak.oakland.edu

Path:

/pub2/macintosh/

✳✳✳

MACWEB (BROWSER)

Anonymous FTP:

Address:

ftp.einet.net

Path:

/einet/mac/macweb/macweb.latest.sea.hqx

✳✳✳

MICROSOFT CORP.

Anonymous FTP:

Address:

ftp.microsoft.com/

***

NET ETHICS

Anonymous FTP:

Address:

nic.merit.edu

Path:

/documents/rfc/rfc1087.txt

***

NET ETIQUETTE GUIDE

Anonymous FTP:

Address:

ftp.sura.net

Path:

/pub/nic/internet.literature/netiquette.txt

***

CHAPTER 7 · HOMESCHOOL RESOURCE DIRECTORY

ONLINE ARCHIVES

FOR AOL

Anonymous FTP:

Address:

ftp.aol.com/

FOR PC

Anonymous FTP:

Address:

ftp.wustl.edu

Path:

/systems/ibmpc/

***

SOFTWARE ARCHIVE SITES

Anonymous FTP:

Address:

export.lcs.mit.edu

Path:

/pub/

Address:

ftp.cc.utexas.edu

Path:

/pub/

Address:

ftp.funet.fi

Path:

/pub/

Cooking

COOKING

Cooking discussions and recipes, where families can find resources for home economics home studies.

alt.cooking-chat

***

RECIPE ARCHIVES

Anonymous FTP:

Address:
gatekeeper.dec.com
Path:

/pub/recipes

Address:

mthvax.cs.miami.edu

Path:

/pub/recipes

Address:

ftp.neosoft.com

Path:

/pub/rec.food/recipes

Address:

cs.ubc.ca

Path:

/pub/local/RECIPES

***

Music

CHRISTIAN MUSIC

An unmoderated group with a stated purpose to focus on Christian music.

rec.music.Christian

✳✳✳

GUITAR CHORDS/TABLATURE

Anonymous FTP:

Address:

ftp.nevada.edu

Path:

/pub/guitar

Address:

131.216.1.11

Path:

/pub/guitar

Address:

ftp.uu.net

✳✳✳

INTRODUCTION TO MUSIC EDUCATION

MUSIC 140. Introduction to Music Education. Introduces basic issues and principles of music education and teaching. Includes 16 hours of early field experience in the teaching of music. 2 hours.

URL:http://www.uiuc.edu/admin_manual/Courses/C_D/ MUSIC140.html

CHAPTER 7 · HOMESCHOOL RESOURCE DIRECTORY

Education

ACADEMY ONE

http://www.nptn.org/cyber.serv/AOneP/academy_one/menu.html

✳✳✳

ALTERNATIVE APPROACHES TO LEARNING

Discussing all aspects of alternative and new approaches to education and learning.

Address:

altlearn.@sjuvm.stjohns.edu

Subscription Address:

listserv@sjuvm.stjohns.edu

✳✳✳

ASK PROF. MATHS

Proffesor Tim Kurtz is Prof. Maths. He encourages students K-9 to submit questions. He will respond dirctly to each question.

Include with your message: problem, name, grade level, and e-mail address on the subject line: state K-5 or 6-9 Address:

maths@sbu.edu

✳✳✳

ART EDUCATION

For the discussion of art education.

k12.ed.art

✲✲✲

BARTLETT'S FAMILIAR QUOTATIONS

http://www.columbia.edu/~svl2/bartlett/

✲✲✲

BEST OF THE K12 INTERNET RESOURCES

A collection of some of what the Internet has to offer in K12 resources. Files and lesson plans can be downloaded.

gopher://informns.k12.mn.us:70/11/best-k12

✲✲✲

CURRICULUM MATERIALS AND I DEAS

A collection of pointers to curriculum resources on the Net. Included are curriculum guides and lesson plans from Ask ERIC.

gopher://gopher.cua.edu

Choose:

Special Resources|Eric Clearinghouse on Assesment and Evaluation|Curriculum Guides, lesson plans, ideas, & resources.

✲✲✲

CYBERSPACE MIDDLE SCHOOL

http://www.scri.fsu.edu/~dennisl/topics/topics.html

❊❊❊

DAILY REPORT CARD

Provides up to date info on the status of educational concerns in the US. From NYSERNet

gopher://nysernet.org

Choose:

Special Collections: Empire Internet Schoolhouse (k-12)|School Reform and Technology planning center|daily report card news service.

❊❊❊

DAILY REPORT NEWS SERVICE

Summarizes information and news in the world of K12 education.

gopher://copernicus.bbn.com:70/11/k12/drc

❊❊❊

EARLY CHILDHOOD EDUCATION ONLINE

Hints for parents and teachers created by a group of early childhood educators.

gopher://gopher.cic.net:3005/00/listservs/early-child-hood-education

❊❊❊

CHAPTER 7 · HOMESCHOOL RESOURCE DIRECTORY

EDUCATION TESTING SERVICE

College credit for High School students. Offers testing for students to earn college credit while in H.S.

gopher://gopher.ets.org:70/11/ets.tests/collegeb/ap

✳✳✳

EISENHOWER NATIONAL CLEARINGHOUSE

The US Dept. of Education funds this gopher which provides a catalog of lesson plans, interactive resources, and software for math and science.

gopher://enc.org

✳✳✳

EMPIRE INTERNET SCHOOLHOUSE

An electronic grab-bag for Internet newcomers with an extensive server offering in K12 resources.

gopher://nysernet.org:3000

✳✳✳

EXPLORATORIUM

Information and resources from the Exploratorium.

gopher://gopher.exploratorium.edu

✳✳✳

ECENET-L

Early childhhod education (preschool to 8).

Subscription Address:

listserv@uiucvmd.bitnet

***

EDUCATION MAILING LISTS

Vocnet is about vocational education.

Address:

vocnet@cmsa.berkeley.edu

Subscription Address:

listserv@cmsa.berkeley.edu

School-l is about primary and post-primary education.

Address:

school-l@irlearn.ucd.ie

Subscription Address:

listserv@irlearn.ucd.ie

***

EDNET

Focusing on issues, projects, news and resources in the field of education.

Address:

ednet@lists.umass.edu

Subscription Address:

listserv@lists.umass.edu

***

ELED-L

For elementary education.

Subscription Address:

listserv@ksuvm.ksu.edu

❋❋❋

GLOBAL SCHOOLHOUSE HOME PAGE

http://k12.cnidr.org/gsh/gshwelcome.html

❋❋❋

EDUCATIONAL RESOURCES: GENERAL RESOURCES

http://www.alaska.net/~steel/edures.html

❋❋❋

GOVERNMENT AGENCIES

Anonymous FTP:

Address:

is.internic.net

Path:

/infosource/internet-info-for-everybody/government-agencies

❋❋❋

HANDS ON CHILDREN'S MUSEUM OF OLYMPIA, WASHINGTON.

The fun place to be, on the Web, for kids 10 years old and under.

http://www.wln.com/~deltapac/hocm.html

✳✳✳

HELPING YOUR CHILD LEARN MATH

With hints and activities to help get you and your kids started.

http://www.ed.gov/pubs/parents/Math/index.html

✳✳✳

KINDERGARTEN TO GRADE 6 CORNER

Interesting facts, things to try, and pen pals for kids to meet.

Address:

gopher://gopher.schoolnet.carleton.ca

Choose:

schoolnet gopherlkindergarten to grade 6 corner

✳✳✳

K-12 SCHOOLS ON THE INTERNET

http://www.geo.arizona.edu/K-12/net.schools.html

✳✳✳

CHAPTER 7 · HOMESCHOOL RESOURCE DIRECTORY

LEGI-SLATE

This is a commercial gopher service that offers texts of thousands of US Congress and other regulatory service documents.

Address:

gopher://gopher.legislate.com

✳✳✳

LESSON PLANS

Address:

gopher://copernicus.bbn.com

Choose:

National School Network Testbed|UCSD InternNet Lesson Plans

✳✳✳

LIBRARY AND INFORMATION SKILLS

Activities and lesson plans aimed at teaching library and information seeking skills.

gopher://ericir.syr.edu:70/11/lesson/SLMAM/skills

✳✳✳

LEARNING DISABILITIES

For the discussion of children with learning disabilities.

alt.support.learning-disab

✳✳✳

MAGIC MATH

Magic Math is a project that encourages k-12 students to use computers to solve math problems and communicate.

To join the list send e-mail to:
with the message: Subscribe Math Magic-your grade here-open

Address:

majordomo@forum.swarthmore.edu

✳✳✳

MATH

For the discussion of technical and mathematical studies.

k12.ed.math

✳✳✳

MATHEMATICS

Address:

gopher://archives.math.utk.edu

✳✳✳

MIDDLE SCHOOL DISCUSSION LIST

A discussion group on and for middle education topics.

Address:

gopher://quest.arc.nasa.gov/0/NASAK-12/teacherres/middle/midschool

✳✳✳

NATIONAL DISTANCE LEARNING CENTER

Supported by Federal funds the NDLC operates this free electronic clearinghouse of learning materials for K12, and supplimentary materials.

gopher://ndlc.occ.uky.edu

❋❋❋

NATIONAL SCHOOL NETWORK

gopher://copernicus.bbn.com:70/11/testbed

❋❋❋

NATIONAL 4-H

The US Department of Agriculture server providing infomation on the 4-H curriculum.

gopher://cyfer.esusda.gov:70/11/cyfer-net/jury/curricula

❋❋❋

NETWORK NUGGETS

News and tips on finding educational resources on the Internet. During the school year updates are e-mailed daily.

To join the list send e-mail to:

Address:

network_nuggets-l@cln.etc.bc.ca

with the message: Sub Network_nuggets-l

Subscription Address:

listserv@cln.etc.bc.ca

❋❋❋

READING ROOM (University of Maryland)

Address:
gopher://info.umd.edu

Choose:
Educational Resources|Academic Reading Room

✳✳✳

SCHOOL RESOURCE MANUAL

Containing more than 100 science, engineering, and teacher resources on the Internet.

Anonymous FTP:

Address:

ftp.ccs.carleton.ca

Path: /pub/schoolnet/manuals/resource

✳✳✳

THE VIRTUAL CLASSROOM

http://indy.inre.asu.edu/~sam/home.html

✳✳✳

SCHOOLHOUSE VIDEOS & CDS

Gives a discount to homeschoolers.

http://www.schoolroom.com/gift/

✳✳✳

SCHOOLSMART

The largest selection of teaching resource materials available in one spot on the Web.

http://www.teachnplay.com/schlsmt.htm

***

THE ANNA STREET ACADEMY

A family homeschool homepage with many resources and lots of helpful homeschool information.

http://www.net-connect.net/~miller/annacad.htm

***

THE LEARNING ZONE

A variety of books, software, charts & maps, games, and tapes that you can order.

http://www.webcom.com/~eyecat/tlz/tlz.html

***

THE ON-LINE EDUCATOR

A "magazine" for educators.

http://www.cris.com/~felixg/OE/index.shtml

***

THE NETSCHOOL

http://netschool.edu/

***

WEBSTER DICTIONARY

http://c.gp.cs.cmu.edu:5103/prog/webster

Science

ACCESS RESEARCH NETWORK HOME PAGE

Many good resources on Creationism.

http://www.arn.org/arn/infopage/info.htm

✳✳✳

ANSWERS IN GENESIS

From the excellent materials by author and speaker Ken Ham.

http://www.ChristianAnswers.net/aig/aighome.html

✳✳✳

ASK MR. SCIENCE

A group of advanced placement students at Christianburg High School are "Mr. Science," and receive questions from K-12 students in science. The students research and respond within 48 hours.

gopher://gopher.cic.net:3005/00/classroom/dr.sci

✳✳✳

BIBLE RESEARCH INSTITUTE PRESENTS SCIENTIFIC CREATIONISM

http://www.goshen.net/BRI/

✳✳✳

CHEMISTRY RESOURCES

http://www.chem.vt.edu/yip/organic/org-home.html

✳✳✳

CHEMISTRY VISUALIZATION PROJECT

The National Science Foundation uses computers and the Internet to help high school students learn difficult concepts in chemistry.

gopher://landrew.ncsa.uiuc.edu:70/1ftp%3Aftp.ncsa.uiuc
.edu@/education/chemviz/

✳✳✳

CREATION/EVOLUTION REFERENCE DATABASE

http://aruba.ccit.arizona.edu/~mooret/cedata.html

✳✳✳

CREATION RESEARCH SOCIETY

http://www.iclnet.org/pub/resources/text/crs/crs-
home.html

✳✳✳

CREATIONISM CONNECTION

http://members.gnn.com/DWReynolds/Creation.html

✳✳✳

DIVINE CREATION VERSUS EVOLUTION

http://203.1.75.10/comm/truth/Creation.html

✳✳✳

EVOLUTION VS. SCICRE (SCIENTIFIC CREATIONISM)

http://www.rtis.com/nat/user/elsberry/evosci.html

✳✳✳

HANDS-ON SCIENCE PROJECTS

The NDN provides curricula and programs for K-12 science.

Address:

gopher://gopher.ed.gov/1/programs/NDN

✳✳✳

ICR

The Institute For Creation Research's home page with many valuable resources.

http://www.icr.org/

✳✳✳

JOHNSON SPACE CENTER

Anonymous FTP:

Address:

krakatoa.jsc.nasa.gov/

✳✳✳

LAMBERT DOLPHIN'S LIBRARY

A Creationist's resource collection.

http://www.best.com/~dolphin/asstbib.shtml

✳✳✳

ORIGINS THE TRUTH IS OUT THERE

http://www.pacificrim.net/~nuanda/origins/Origins.html

✳✳✳

PERIODIC TABLE OF ELEMENTS

http://www.cchem.berkeley.edu/Table/index.html

✳✳✳

REASONS TO BELIEVE

Hugh Ross' organization.

http://www.surf.com/reasons/

✳✳✳

(SEDS) STUDENTS FOR THE EXPLORATION AND DEVELOPMENT OF SPACE

Anonymous FTP:

Address:

ftp.seds.lpl.arizona.edu/

✳✳✳

SCIENCE

Anonymous FTP:

Address:

ftp.bio.indiana.edu//

***

USENET NEWSGROUP

For the discussion of scientific studies.

k12.ed.science

***

SCIENCE & CHRISTIANITY MAILING LIST

http://hercules.geology.uiuc.edu/%7Eschimmri/christiani-ty/scichr.html

***

THE CENTER FOR SCIENTIFIC CREATION

http://www.indirect.com/www/wbrown/

***

WELCOME TO TALK.ORIGINS

An archive homepage based on the heated debate located in Usenet.

http://rumba.ics.uci.edu:8080/

***

Social Studies

SOCIAL STUDIES

For the discussion of social studies.

k12.ed.soc-studies

※※※

SCOUT REPORT: NEW INTERNET RESOURCES

A weekly guide to what's the best of recently announced education and research resources on the Internet.

To join the list send e-mail to:

with the message: Subscribe Scout Report

Subscription Address:

mojordomo@dstest.internic.net

※※※

SPECIAL EDUCATION

Network with others interested in current practices, policies and new developments.

To join the list send e-mail to:

Address:

spedtalk@virginia.edu

Subscription Address:

majordomo@virginia.edu

※※※

STUDENT FINANCIAL AID ADMINISTRATION

To join the list send e-mail to:

Address:

finaid-l@psuvm.psu.edu

Subscription Address:

listserv@psuvm.psu.edu

✳✳✳

SUPREME COURT DECISIONS

Anonymous FTP:

Address:

ftp.cwru.edu

✳✳✳

TECHNICAL/VOCATIONAL

For the discussion of technical and vocational studies.

k12.ed.tech

✳✳✳

TECHNOLOGY AND INFORMATION EDUCATION SERVICES (TIES)

A gopher providing many K12 educational resources.

Address:

gopher://tiesnet.ties.k12.mn.us

✳✳✳

CHAPTER 7 · HOMESCHOOL RESOURCE DIRECTORY

TALENTED AND GIFTED

Programs for children who show exceptional skill, intelligence or creativity are discussed.

To join the list send e-mail to:

Address:

tag-l@vm1.nodak.edu

Subscription Address

listserv@vm1.nodak.edu

***

US DEPARTMENT OF EDUCATION

Includes programs, goals, announcements of the D of E, as well as educational Software.

 Gopher Address:

gopher://gopher.ed.gov

***

 Anonymous FTP:

Address:

ftp.ed.gov

Path:

/gopher/

***

U.S. NATIONAL K12 GOPHER

For the experimentation with applications that bring new educational benefits.

Address:

gopher://copernicus.bbn.com

✳✳✳

U.S. SENATE

A gopher offering full text searches for all Senate documents.

Address:

gopher://gopher.senate.gov/11

✳✳✳

VOCATIONAL EDUCATION

Network with administrators of Vocational Education Systems. Find out how to use the Internet to enhance the learning environment.

USENET:

bit.listserv.vocnet

E-MAIL:

To join the list send e-mail to:

vocnet@ucbcmsa.bitnet

Subscription Address:

listserv@ucbcmsa.bitnet

✳✳✳

CHAPTER 7 · HOMESCHOOL RESOURCE DIRECTORY

Children & Parents

BRINGING UP BABY

Taken from a weekly question-and-answer column written by Martha Erickson, this is a collection of short articles on child rearing questions.

Address:

gopher://tinman.mes.umn.edu.:80/11/resources/children/shortarticles/BringingupBaby

***

KIDS & COMPUTERS

Discussion about kids and computers.

misc.kids.computers

***

KIDS TOPICS

misc.kids.info

***

LEGOS NEWSGROUP

rec.toys.lego

***

CHILDREN'S ART BOOKS

rec.arts.books.childrens

✳✳✳

CHILDREN'S BOOKS

About children's literature.

rec.arts.books.childrens

✳✳✳

KIDLINK

A mailing list for planning activities for younger network users.

To join the list send e-mail to:

Address:

kidlink@vm1.nodak.edu

Subscription Address:

listserv@vm1.nodak.edu

✳✳✳

KIDOPEDIA

A global online encyclopedia written by and for kids.

Address: kidpedia@sjuvm.stjohns.edu

Subscription Address:

listserv@sjuvm.stjohns.edu

✳✳✳

CHAPTER 7 · HOMESCHOOL RESOURCE DIRECTORY

ROYAL RANGERS

Group organized to support youth and discuss youth-related activities.

alt.org.Royal-Rangers

✻✻✻

SOC.RELIGION.CHRISTIAN.YOUTH-WORK

News, issues, and guidance related to youth and working with youth.

soc.Religion.Christian.Youth-Work

✻✻✻

PARENTING SOLUTIONS

Discussion on parenting issues.

alt.parenting.solutions

✻✻✻

Christian Resources

CHRISTIAN BIBLE STUDY

Moderated discussion on Christian Bible Study.

soc.Religion.Christian.Bible-Study

✳✳✳

CHRISTIAN ANSWERS NETWORK

Christian Answers Network provides answers to over 100 of today's most important questions on many Christian family issues.

http://www.christiananswers.net

✳✳✳

CHRISTIAN DISCUSSION

A list for Christians to discuss issues and information.

To join the list send e-mail to:

Address:

christian@grian.cps.altadens.ca.us

Subscription Address:

christian-request@grian.cps.altadena.ca.us

✳✳✳

CHRISTIAN LEADERSHIP FORUM

Meet other Christian leaders and share concerns, problems, ideas and insights.

To join the list send e-mail to:

Address:

leadership@iclnet93.iclnet.org

Subscription Address:

majordomo@iclnet93.iclnet.org

✳✳✳

CHRISTIANITY NEWSGROUPS

Discuss and debate important topics on Christianity.

alt.christnet

alt.christnet.philosophy

alt.christnet.theology

alt.religion.christian

✳✳✳

CHRISTIAN RESOURCES

Anonymous FTP:

Address:

iclnet93.iclnet.org

Path:

/pub/resources/christian-resources.txt

✳✳✳

 EARLY CHURCH DOCUMENTS

Anonymous FTP:

Address:

iclnet93.iclnet.org

Path:

/pub/resources/christian-history.html

✳✳✳

 GODLY GRAPHICS ARCHIVES

Anonymous FTP:

Address:

ftp.cybernetics.net

Path:

/pub/users/adamb

✳✳✳

SOC.RELIGION.CHRISTIAN.BIBLE-STUDY ARCHIVE

Anonymous FTP:

Address:

ftp.spss.com

Path:

/pub/bible

✳✳✳

CHAPTER 7 · HOMESCHOOL RESOURCE DIRECTORY

SUNSITE ARCHIVES

From the University of North Carolina, contains: The Online Bible *version 6.11 and more.*

Anonymous FTP:

Address:

sunsite.unc.edu

Path:

/pub/academic/religious_studies/bible.old

***

History

 ARCHI-GOPHER (Architecture and Fine Arts)

Images and writings about architecture and other fine arts.

Address:

gopher://libra.arch.umich.edu

✳✳✳

 CIVIL WAR

Discussion about the American Civil War.

alt.war.civil.usa

✳✳✳

 HISTORY

For the discussion of history.

alt.history-living

✳✳✳

English & Literature

ACRONYM/BY/MAIL

A free service, offered by "wordserver," unravels acronyms by e-mail. Include the message: Acronym (and the acronym whose expansion you need to know)
Address:

wsmith@wordsmith.org

✳✳✳

A·WORD·A·DAY

A great Internet tool to slowly but surely improve your English vocabulary.

To join the list send e-mail to:

Address:

linguaphile@wordsmith.org

Subscription Address:

wsmith@wordsmith.org

✳✳✳

CHILDREN'S LITERATURE AND FAIRY TALES

Find the full texts of children's literature and fables such as Aesop's fables on this gopher.
Address:

gopher://unix5.nysed.gov:70/11/k-12%20resources/english-language%20arts/children%27s%20Lit%20%26%20fairy%20tales

✳✳✳

CREWRT-L

For the discussion of creative writing in education.

Subscription Address:

listserv@mizzou1.missouri.edu

✳✳✳

DICTIONARY/BY/MAIL

A free service, offered by "wordserver," to look up definitions of words by e-mail. Include the message: info dictionary/by/mail (with the word you need defined)
Address:

wsmith@wordsmith.org

✳✳✳

ENGLISH USAGE

alt.english.usage

✳✳✳

LANGUAGE/ENGLISH NEWSGROUP

misc.education.language.english

✳✳✳

JOURNALISM

For journalists and journalism students.

alt.journalism

ONLINE WRITING LAB (OWL)

A place to find tips and tutoring in grammar and composition, as well as research sources.

To join the list send e-mail to:

Address:

owl@sage.cc.purdue.edu

With the message: owl-request

✳✳✳

QUALITY OF EDUCATION LISTSERV

A forum for parents, teachers, and students concerned with issues relating to the quality of, and alternatives for education.

To join the list send e-mail to:

Address:

BGEDU-L@UKCC.BITNET

with the message: SUBBGEDU-L

Subscription Address:

listserv@UKCC.UKY.EDU

✳✳✳

QUOTATIONS

Discover the origin of famous quotes.

alt.quotations

✳✳✳

RHYME-N-REASON

A new challenge awaits each day via e-mail presented by "wordserver's" Rhyme-n-Reason.

To join the list send e-mail to:
Address:

wsmith@wordsmith.org

With the message: Rhyme-n-Reason Today

✳✳✳

THESAURUS/BY/MAIL

A PLACE TO FIND THE SYNONYMS FOR ANY WORD BY USING AN ONLINE VERSION OF ROGET'S THESAURUS.

To join the list send e-mail to:

Address:

wsmith@lrdc5.lrdc.pitt.edu

With the message: Synonym (the word whose synonym you want to find)

✳✳✳

WRITING

For the discussion of writing methods and skills, and information on writing resources.

misc.writing

✳✳✳

CHAPTER 7 · HOMESCHOOL RESOURCE DIRECTORY

Service Providers

COMMUNITY NETWORKS

Anonymous FTP:

Address:

netcom.com

Path:

/pub/amcgee/community/communet.msg

✳✳✳

FREENETS

Free public Internet access.

alt.online-service.freenet

✳✳✳

LIST OF FREENETS

An extensive collection of leads to freenets around the world.

Name: List of FreeNets
Address:

gopher://acs.eku.edu:70/11disk%24acs%3A%5B00600
6.gopherd.gopher_data.tunnels.free%5D

✳✳✳

INTERNET SERVICES

Lists and discussions on Internet providers.

alt.internet.services

***

INTERNET ACCESS GUIDE

Anonymous FTP:

Address:

nic.merit.edu

Path:

/introducing.the.internet/access.guide

***

ONLINE NEWSGROUPS

Discussion about major online services.

Large Commercial Online Services:

alt.online-service

America Online:

alt.online-service.america-online

CompuServe:

alt.online-service.compuserve

Delphi:

alt.online-service.delphi

Prodigy:

alt.online-service.prodigy

***

CHAPTER 7 · HOMESCHOOL RESOURCE DIRECTORY

Newbies

NEWBIES

For those new to the Internet.

alt.newbies

***

NEWBIE NEWZ

Find out what you need to know to get started on the Internet. A special mailing list designed for "newbies." Questions are encouraged about "rules of the road" or directions navigating the Information Superhighway.

To join the list send e-mail to:

Address: NewbieNewz@IO.com

with the message: Subscribe NewbieNewz and e-mail address.

Subscription Address: NewbieNews-request@IO.com

***

LET'S LEARN

Educational fun and games on the Internet for newbies, this gopher provides a slow and easy introduction to the network.

Address:

gopher://gopher.oise.on.ca:70/11/resources/IRes4Ed/re
sources/fun/educational

***

SCAVENGER HUNT (Schoolnet Gopher)

A fun way to learn with the Internet by following these scavenger hunts geared for school age kids.

Address:

gopher://gopher.schoolnet.carleton.ca

Choose:

schoolnet gopher|virtual school|recess|scavenger hunts

***

SURFING THE INTERNET

Anonymous FTP:

Address:

nysernet.org

Path:

/pub/resources/guides/surfing.2.0.3.txt

***

APPENDIX A

Internet Service Providers

I f you've come this far, there's a good chance that you're ready (or soon to be ready) to locate and sign up with a local ISP. For $20 to $25 a month (in most cases) you'll be able to spend as much time online as you like—or as long as you choose to allow—without paying expensive long-distance telephone charges. While this route costs more than a $9.95-per-month online membership, you could realize a substantial savings if you and your family spend an average of 20 minutes a day or more online.

✔ *See pages 112–113 for Internet addresses to find additional Internet Service Providers and "freenets" around the world.*

There are thousands of service providers around the country, but we've listed five from each state to get you started. If you do not find your area code listed, don't despair! This is by no means a comprehensive list, and local ISPs are popping up all over—even in rural areas. Check with your local library, high school, community college, or university. Ask for someone in the computer department, and find out where they call for their internet connection. You may discover that the institution itself provides limited internet service, with a small number of free connections available to the general public. Another likely source of information is the nearest computer store, or the classifieds in your local paper.

Alabama

CHENEY COMMUNICATIONS COMPANY
Area Codes: 205, 800
e-mail: info@cheney.net
Phone: (800) CHENEY-1
URL: http://www.cheney.net/

COMMUNITY INTERNET CONNECT, INC.
Area Codes: 205
e-mail: info@cici.com
Phone: (205) 722-0199
URL: http://www.cici.com/homepage.html/

HIWAAY INFORMATION SERVICES
Area Codes: 205
e-mail: info@HiWAAY.net
Phone: (205) 533-3131 ext. 5
URL: http://www.hiwaay.net/

LIGHTSPEED DATA LINKS, INC.
Area Codes: 205, 706
e-mail: info@ldl.net
Phone: (706) 321-1261
URL: http://www.ldl.net/

**WSNETWORK COMMUNICATIONS SERVICES, INC.
(WSNETWORK)**
Area Codes: 205, 334
e-mail: info@wsnet.com
Phone: (800) INET-750
URL: http://www.wsnet.com/

Alaska

CORCOM, INC.
Area Codes: 907
e-mail: support@corcom.com
Phone: (907) 563-1191
URL: http://www.corcom.com/

IMAGINET, INC.
Area Codes: 907
e-mail: coppick@imagi.net
Phone: (907) 455-9638
URL: http://www.imagi.net/

INTERNET ALASKA
Area Codes: 907
e-mail: info@alaska.net
e-mail: support@alaska.net
Phone: (907) 562-4638
URL: http://www.alaska.net/

MATNET, INC.
Area Codes: 907
e-mail: admin@matnet.com
Phone: (907) 373-3580
URL: http://www.matnet.com/

NORTHWESTNET
Area Codes: 206, 208, 360, 406, 503, 509, 701, 907
e-mail: info@nwnet.net
Phone: (206) 562-3000
URL: http://www.nwnet.net/

Arizona

AMUG
Area Codes: 602
e-mail: emod@amug.org
Phone: (602) 553-8966
URL: http://www.amug.org/

CROSSROADS COMMUNICATIONS
Area Codes: 602
e-mail: info@xroads.com
Phone: (602) 813-9040
URL: http://www.xroads.com/

EVERGREEN INTERNET (EVERGREEN CYBERMART, EVERGREEN CYBERWEB)
Area Codes: 303, 602, 702, 801
e-mail: evergreen@enet.net
Phone: (602) 926-4500
URL: http://cybermart.com/

INTERNET ACCESS OF ARIZONA
Area Codes: 602
e-mail: info@neta.com
Phone: (602) 820-4000
URL: http://www.neta.com/

PRIMENET
Area Codes: 520, 602
e-mail: info@primenet.com
Phone: (800) 4-NET-FUN
URL: http://www.primenet.com/

Arkansas

ARISTOTLE INTERNET ACCESS

Area Codes: 501
e-mail: info@aristotle.net
Phone: (501) 374-4638
URL: http://www.aristotle.net/

AXESS PROVIDERS

Area Codes: 501
e-mail: info@axs.net
Phone: (501) 225-6901 (Little Rock)
(501) 327-0096 (Conway)
URL: http://www.axs.net/

INTERNET PARTNERS OF AMERICAS

Area Codes: 417, 501, 713
e-mail: info@ipa.net
Phone: (800) 785-4091
URL: http://www.ipa.net/

MIDNET

Area Codes: 314, 316, 402, 405, 501, 515, 605, 816,
913, 918
e-mail: sales@mid.net
Phone: (800) 682-5550
URL: http://www.mid.net/

YOURNET

Area Codes: 501
e-mail: newuser@yournet.com
Phone: (501) 741-0943
URL: http://www.yournet.com/

California

ABLECOM

Area Codes: 408, 415, 510
e-mail: support@ablecom.net
Phone: (408) 280-1000
URL: http://www.ablecom.net/

APPENDIX A · INTERNET SERVICE PROVIDERS

ADVANCED NETWORK SOLUTIONS

Area Codes: 805, 818
e-mail: info@adnetsol.com
Phone: (805) 446-2219
URL: http://www.adnetsol.com/

LIGHTSIDE, INC.

Area Codes: 310, 714, 818, 909
e-mail: lightside@lightside.net
Phone: (818) 858-9261
URL: http://www.lightside.net/

SACRAMENTO NETWORK ACCESS, INC.

Area Codes: 209, 415, 800, 916
e-mail: ghall@sna.com
Phone: (916) 565-4500
URL: http://www.sna.com/

VISICOM NETWORK SERVICES, "THE NETWORK CONNECTION"

Area Codes: 619
e-mail: frances@tncnet.com
Phone: (619) 457-2111 x248
URL: http://www.tncnet.com/

Colorado

COLORADO SUPERNET, INC.

Area Codes: 303, 719, 800, 970
e-mail: info@csn.net
Phone: (303) 296-8202
URL: http://www.csn.net/

FRONT RANGE INTERNET, INC.

Area Codes: 303, 719, 970
e-mail: info@frii.com
Phone: (970) 224-3668
URL: http://www.frii.com/

INTERNET EXPRESS

Area Codes: 206, 303, 505, 602, 719, 800
e-mail: service@usa.net
Phone: (800) 592-1240
URL: http://www.usa.net/

ROCKY MOUNTAIN INTERNET, INC

Area Codes: 303, 719, 970

e-mail: info@rmii.com

Phone: (800) 900-RMII

SUPERNET, INC.

Area Codes: 303, 719, 800, 970

e-mail: info@csn.net

Phone: (303) 296-8202

URL: http://www.csn.net/

Connecticut

CENTNET, INC.

Area Codes: 203, 207, 401, 413, 508, 603, 617, 802

e-mail: info@cent.net

Phone: (617) 492-6079

URL: http:/www.control.com/centnet/

COMPUTERIZED HORIZONS

Area Codes: 203

e-mail: sysop@fcc.com

Phone: (203) 335-7431

URL: http://fcc.com/

MIRACOM

Area Codes: 203

e-mail: sales@miracle.net

Phone: (203) 523-5677

URL: http://www.miracle.net/

NETPLEX

Area Codes: 203

e-mail: info@ntplx.net

Phone: (203) 233-1111

URL: http://www.ntplx.net/

TIAC

Area Codes: 202, 203, 212, 508, 603, 617

e-mail: info@tiac.net

Phone: (617) 276-7200

URL: http://www.tiac.net/

Delaware

BUSINESS DATA SYSTEMS, INC.
Area Codes: 302, 410, 610
e-mail: info@bdsnet.com
Phone: (302) 674-2840
URL: http://www.bdsnet.com/

DEL LINK INC.
Area Codes: 302, 610, 717
e-mail: info@cpcnet.com
Phone: (302) 892-5927
(800) 770-SURF
URL: http://boss.cpcnet.com/

DELMARVA ONLINE!
Area Codes: 302, 410
e-mail: admin@dmv.com
Phone: (410) 749-7898
URL: http://www.dmv.com/

PREPNET
Area Codes: 215, 302, 412, 610, 717, 814
e-mail: nic@prep.net
Phone: (412) 267-7870
URL: http://www.prep.net/

SSNET, INC.
Area Codes: 302, 410, 610
e-mail: sharris@ssnet.com
russ@ssnet.com
Phone: (302) 378-1386
URL: http://ssnet.com/

Florida

ALL WORLD NETWORK, INC.
Area Codes: 813
e-mail: info@allworld.com
Phone: (813) 988-7772
URL: http://www.allworld.com/

AUGLINK COMMUNICATIONS, INC.
Area Codes: 904
e-mail: captdave@aug.com
Phone: (904) 824 1660
URL: http://www.aug.com/

BRIDGENET, LC
Area Codes: 305
e-mail: sales@bridge.net
Phone: (305) 374-3031
URL: http://www.bridge.net/

CENTURION TECHNOLOGIES OF TAMPA BAY
Area Codes: 813, 941
e-mail: info@tpa.cent.com
Phone: (813) 538 1919
URL: http://tpa.cent.com/

TACHYON COMMUNICATIONS CORP.
Area Codes: 407
e-mail: scpayne@tach.net
Phone: (407) 728-8081
URL: http://www.tach.net/

Georgia

ALTERNET - UUNET
Area Codes: 212, 214, 310, 404, 408, 415, 503, 510, 617, 703, 713, 800, 908
e-mail: info@alter.net
Phone: (800) 488-6384
URL: http://www.alter.net/

AMERICA NET
Area Codes: 404, 770
e-mail: sales@america.net
Phone: (770) 667-7200
URL: http://www.america.net/

FIRST NET
Area Codes: 904, 912
e-mail: support@jax.gulfnet.com
Phone: (904) 743-7686
URL: http://jax.gulfnet.com/

NETDEPOT, INC.

Area Codes: 404, 770, 910
e-mail: info@netdepot.com
Phone: (404) 434-5595

VIPER COMPUTER SYSTEMS, INC. (VIPERNET)

Area Codes: 205, 334, 706, 800
e-mail: vipersys@viper.net
Phone: (334) 826-1912
(800) VIPER-96
URL: http://www.viper.net/

Hawaii

FLEX INFORMATION NETWORK

Area Codes: 808
e-mail: postmaster@aloha.com
Phone: (808) 539-3790

HAWAII INTERNET TECHNOLOGY SOLUTIONS

Area Codes: 808
e-mail: info@hits.net
Phone: (808) 532-8227
URL: http://www.hits.net/

HAWAII ONLINE (HOL)

Area Codes: 808
e-mail: info@aloha.net
Phone: (800) 207-1880
(808) 533-6981
URL: http://www.aloha.net/ or http://planet-hawaii.com/

LAVANET

Area Codes: 808
e-mail: info@lava.net
Phone: (808) 545-5282
URL: http://www.lava.net/

MAUI GLOBAL COMMUNICATIONS CO., MAUI NET

Area Codes: 808
e-mail: info@maui.net
Phone: (808) 875-2535
URL: http://www.maui.net/

Idaho

COMPUTECH (INTERNET ENGINEERING ASSOCIATES, IEA.COM)
Area Codes: 208, 509
e-mail: info@iea.com
Phone: (509) 624-6798
(800) 784-3217
URL: http://www.iea.com/

DMI COMPUTERS / DMI COMPUTER GRAPHICS
Area Codes: 208, 509, 800
e-mail: randyo@dmi.net
Phone: (800) 775-1340
URL: http://www.dmi.net/

IDAHO COMPUTER SERVICES, INC.
Area Codes: 208
e-mail: ics@magiclink.com
Phone: (208) 734-2245
URL: http://www.magiclink.com/

NORTHWESTNET
Area Codes: 206, 208, 360, 406, 503, 509, 701, 907
e-mail: info@nwnet.net
Phone: (206) 562-3000
URL: http://www.nwnet.net/

TRIBUNE INTERNET SERVICES
Area Codes: 208, 509
e-mail: gc@moscow.com
Phone: (208) 743-9411
URL: http://www.lmtribune.com/

Illinois

ALLIED ACCESS, INC.
Area Codes: 314, 502, 618, 800
e-mail: sales@intrnet.net
Phone: (800) 463-8366
URL: http://www.internet.net/

AMERICAN INFORMATION SYSTEMS
Area Codes: 312, 708, 815
e-mail: info@ais.net
Phone: (312) 255-8500
URL: http://www.ais.net/

CICNET

Area Codes: 312, 313, 708, 800
e-mail: info@cic.net
Phone: (800) 947-4754
URL: http://www.cic.net/

NETWAVE(SM)

Area Codes: 312, 708
e-mail: info@maui.netwave.net
Phone: (800) 961-WAVE
URL: http://www.netwave.net/info.html/

WORLDWIDE ACCESS

Area Codes: 312, 708
e-mail: info@wwa.com
Phone: (708) 367-1870
(312) 803-9921
URL: http://www.wwa.com/

Indiana

AUTOMATED DATA

Area Codes: 219
e-mail: Kirk@adsnet.com
Phone: (219) 879-6600

BLUEGRASSNET

Area Codes: 317, 502, 513, 606, 615, 812
e-mail: info@bluegrass.net
Phone: (502) 589-INET
URL: http://www.bluegrass.net/

CUSTOM LOGIC SYSTEMS

Area Codes: 219
e-mail: info@cl-sys.com
Phone: (219) 255-5201
URL: http://www.cl-sys.com/

PLA-NET, INC.

Area Codes: 219
e-mail: wahlberg@pla-net.net
Phone: (219) 756-1675
URL: http://www.pla-net.net/

WINK COMMUNICATIONS
Area Codes: 219, 312, 414, 630, 708, 815
e-mail: sales@winkcomm.com
Phone: (708) 310-WINK
URL: http://www.winkcomm.com/

Iowa

AMESNET, INC.
Area Codes: 515
e-mail: sysop@ames.net
Phone: (515) 233-8956
URL: http://www.ames.net/

CEDARNET
Area Codes: 319
e-mail: seans@www.cedarnet.com
Phone: (319) 390-0650
URL: http://www.cedarnet.com/

CYBERSPACE
Area Codes: 206, 515
e-mail: info@cyberspace.com
Phone: (206) 505-5577
URL: http://www.cyberspace.com/

INTERNET NAVIGATOR INC.
Area Codes: 319
e-mail: support@inav.net
Phone: (319) 626-7464
URL: http://www.inav.net/

QUAD-CITIES ONLINE
Area Codes: 309, 319
e-mail: sysop@qconline.com
Phone: (309) 757-5037
URL: http://www.qconline.com/

Kansas

ACCUNET, INC.
Area Codes: 816, 913
e-mail: dwhitten@accunet.com
Phone: (816) 246-9094
URL: http://www.accunet.com/

DATABANK, INC.
Area Codes: 202, 301, 316, 703, 800, 816, 913, 914
e-mail: info@databank.com
Phone: (913) 842-6699
URL: http://www.databank.com/

FUTURE NET, INC.
Area Codes: 316
e-mail: info@fn.net
Phone: (316) 652-0070
URL: http://www.fn.net/

TYRELL CORPORATION
Area Codes: 316, 504, 816, 913
e-mail: info@tyrell.net
Phone: (800) TYRELL-1
 URL: http://www.tyrell.net/

UNICOM COMMUNICATIONS
Area Codes: 913
e-mail: fyi@unicom.net
Phone: (913) 383-1983
URL: http://www.unicom.net/

Kentucky

ALLIED ACCESS, INC.
Area Codes: 314, 502, 618, 800
e-mail: sales@intrnet.net
Phone: (800) 463-8366
URL: http://www.internet.net/

IGLOU INTERNET SERVICES
Area Codes: 502, 513, 606, 812
e-mail: info@iglou.com
Phone: (502) 966-3848
(800) I-DO-IGLOU
URL: http://www.iglou.com/

ONENET COMMUNICATIONS
Area Codes: 513, 606, 800
e-mail: info@one.net
Phone: (513) 326-6000
URL: http://www.one.net/

RAM TECHNOLOGIES

Area Codes: 304, 606, 614,
e-mail: info@ramlink.net
Phone: (800) 950-8878
URL: http://www.ramlink.net/

SOUTHERN KY NETWORK

Area Codes: 502, 606, 615
e-mail: admin@skn.net
Phone: (606) 877-1283
URL: http://www.skn.net/

Louisiana

ACCESSCOM INTERNET PROVIDERS

Area Codes: 504
e-mail: info@accesscom.net
Phone: (504) 887-0022
URL: http://www.accesscom.net/

THE BIG EASY

Area Codes: 504
e-mail: info@bigeasy.com
Phone: (800) 819-4847
URL: http://www.bigeasy.com/

COMMUNIQUE, INC.

Area Codes: 504
e-mail: info@communique.net
Phone: (504) 527-6200
URL: http://www.communique.net/

INTERNODE, INC.

Area Codes: 504
e-mail: info@NTERnode.com
Phone: (504) 524-3455
URL: http://www.nternode.com/

TYRELL CORPORATION

Area Codes: 316, 504, 816, 913
e-mail: info@tyrell.net
Phone: (816) 459-7584
(800) TYRELL-1
URL: http://www.tyrell.net/

Maine

ACADIANET
Area Codes: 207
e-mail: dirvin@acadia.net
Phone: (207) 288-5959
URL: http://home.acadia.net/

BIDDEFORD INTERNET
Area Codes: 207
e-mail: staff@biddeford.com
Phone: (207) 286-3265
URL: http://www.biddeford.com/

CENTNET, INC.
Area Codes: 203, 207, 401, 413, 508, 603, 617, 802
e-mail: info@cent.net
Phone: (617) 492-6079
URL: http:/www.control.com/centnet/

INTERNET MAINE INC.
Area Codes: 207
e-mail: mtenney@mainelink.net
Phone: (207) 780-0416
URL: http://www.mainelink.net/

MV COMMUNICATIONS, INC.
Area Codes: 207, 508, 603
e-mail: mv-admin@mv.mv.com
Phone: (603) 429-2223
(800) MVC-NETS
URL: http://www.mv.com/

Maryland

AMERICAN INFORMATION NETWORK
Area Codes: 202, 301, 410
e-mail: admin@ai.net
Phone: (410) 715-6808
URL: http://www.ai.net/

ARINTERNET CORPORATION
Area Codes: 202, 301, 410, 703, SprintNet
e-mail: ari@ari.net
Phone: (301) 459-7171
(800) 459-7175
URL: http://www.ari.net/

BUSINESS DATA SYSTEMS, INC.

Area Codes: 302, 410, 610
e-mail: admin@bdsnet.com
Phone: (302) 674-2840
URL: http://www.bdsnet.com/

SMART.NET

Area Codes: 301, 410
e-mail: paulgani@smart.net
Phone: (410) 792-4555
URL: http://www.smart.net/

VIRTUAL NETWORKS INCORPORATED

Area Codes: 202, 301, 410, 703
e-mail: info@vni.net
Phone: (800) 947-0110
URL: http://www.vni.net/

Massachusetts

ADVANCED COMMUNICATION SYSTEMS INC.

Area Codes: 508, 603, 617
e-mail: sales@star.net
Phone: (508) 922-8238
URL: http://www.star.net/

ALTERNET - UUNET

Area Codes: 212, 214, 310, 404, 408, 415, 503, 510,
617, 703, 713, 800, 908
e-mail: sales@alter.net
Phone: (800) 488-6384
URL: http://www.alter.net/

CHELMSFORD ON-LINE

Area Codes: 508
e-mail: cyndiann@chelmsford.com
URL: http://www.chelmsford.com/

EMPIRE.NET, INC.

Area Codes: 508, 603
e-mail: sales@empire.net
Phone: (603) 889-1220
URL: http://www.empire.net/

VINEYARD.NET
Area Codes: 508
e-mail: vni@vineyard.net
Phone: (508) 693-3608
URL: http://vineyard.net/

Michigan

ALLIANCE NETWORK, INC.
Area Codes: 313, 517, 616, 810, 906
e-mail: Terry@Server.Alliance.Net
Phone: (800) 767-4654
URL: http://www.alliance.net/

BRANCH INTERNET SERVICES INC.
Area Codes: 313, 419, 517, 616, 810
e-mail: branch-info@branch.com
Phone: (800) 349-1747
URL: http://branch.com/

COMPUTER NETWORKING SERVICES, INC.
Area Codes: 313, 810
e-mail: Jerryf@compnetserv.com
Phone: (810) 939-8292
URL: http://www.compnetserv.com/

DALE INFORMATION SERVICES
Area Codes: 616
e-mail: pdale@dinfsvs.com
Phone: (616) 527-4747
URL: http://www.dinfsvs.com/

EAGLEQUEST, INC.
Area Codes: 810
e-mail: nick@eaglequest.com
Phone: (810) 650-4700
URL: http://www.eaglequest.com/

Minnesota

AURORA COMMUNICATIONS, INC.
Area Codes: 612
e-mail: info@aurorainc.com
Phone: (612) 224-6465
URL: http://www.aurorainc.com/

BITSTREAM UNDERGROUND
Area Codes: 612
e-mail: gods@bitstream.net
Phone: (612) 321-9290
URL: http://www.bitstream.net/

CLOUDNET
Area Codes: 612
e-mail: info@cloudnet.com
Phone: (612) 240-8243
URL: http://www.cloudnet.com/

VITEX COMMUNICATIONS
Area Codes: 612
e-mail: info@vitex.com
Phone: (612) 822-1166
URL: http://www.vitex.com/

WAVEFRONT COMMUNICATIONS, INC.
Area Codes: 612
e-mail: craig@wavefront.com
Phone: (612) 638-9594
URL: http://www.wavefront.com/

Mississippi

ARIS TECHNOLOGY, INC.
Area Codes: 601
e-mail: info@aris.com
Phone: (601) 324-7638
URL: http://www.aris.com/

DATASYNC INTERNET SERVICES
Area Codes: 334, 601
e-mail: biz-info@datasync.com
Phone: (601) 872-0001
URL: http://www.datasync.com/

INTERNET DOORWAY, INC
Area Codes: 601
e-mail: marketing@netdoor.com
Phone: (800) 952-1570
URL: http://www.netdoor.com/

APPENDIX A · INTERNET SERVICE PROVIDERS

SYNERGY COMMUNICATIONS
Area Codes: 601
e-mail: sales@synergy.net
Phone: (402) 346-4638
URL: http://www.synergy.net/

TECLINK
Area Codes: 601
e-mail: info@TEClink.net
Phone: (601) 949-6992
URL: http://www.teclink.net/

Missouri

ALLIED ACCESS, INC.
Area Codes: 314, 502, 618, 800
e-mail: dellison@intrnet.net
Phone: (618) 684-2255
(800) 463-8366
URL: http://www.internet.net/

CYBERGATE L.L.C.
Area Codes: 314, 618
e-mail: jim@cybergate.org
Phone: (314) 214-1013
(800) 839-9936
URL: http://www.cybergate.org/

DATABANK, INC.
Area Codes: 202, 301, 316, 703, 800, 816, 913, 914
e-mail: support@databank.com
Phone: (913) 842-6699
URL: http://www.databank.com/

GRAPEVINE INTERACTIVE, INC.
Area Codes: 816, 913
e-mail: support@kc.grapevine.com
Phone: (913) 438-6600
URL: http://www.grapevine.com/

ICON - A SERVICE OF SAINT LOUIS INTERNET CONNECTIONS, LLC
Area Codes: 314
e-mail: info@icon-stl.net
Phone: (314) 241-4266
URL: http://www.icon-stl.net/

Montana

INTERMOUNTAIN INTERNET CORP.

Area Codes: 406
e-mail: jeb@initco.net
Phone: (800) 966-3930
URL: http://www.initco.net/

INTERNET SERVICES MONTANA, INC.

Area Codes: 406
e-mail: support@ism.net
Phone: (406) 542-0838
URL: http://www.ism.net/

MONTANA INTERNET COOPERATIVE

Area Codes: 406
e-mail: admin@mt.net
Phone: (406) 443-3347
URL: http://www.mt.net/

NETRIX INTERNET SYSTEM DESIGN, INC.

Area Codes: 406
e-mail: leesa@netrix.net
Phone: (406) 257-4638
URL: http://www.netrix.net/

NORTHWESTNET

Area Codes: 206, 208, 360, 406, 503, 509, 701, 907
e-mail: info@nwnet.net
Phone: (206) 562-3000
URL: http://www.nwnet.net/

Nebraska

INS INFO SERVICES

Area Codes: 319, 402, 515, 712, 800
e-mail: info@netins.net
Phone: (515) 830-0110
(800) 546-6587
URL: http://www.netins.net/

INTERNET NEBRASKA

Area Codes: 402
e-mail: manager@inetnebr.com
Phone: (402) 434-8680
URL: http://www.inetnebr.com/

MIDNET

Area Codes: 314, 316, 402, 405, 501, 515, 605, 816, 913, 918
e-mail: witts@mid.net
Phone: (800) 682-5550
URL: http://www.mid.net/

NEBRASKA ON-RAMP

Area Codes: 402
e-mail: Info@neonramp.com
Phone: (402) 331-2112
URL: http://neonramp.com/

OMAHA FREE-NET

Area Codes: 402
e-mail: Daliano@unomaha.edu
Phone: (402) 559-5866
URL: http://omahafreetnet.org/

Nevada

ACCESS NEVADA, INC.

Area Codes: 702
e-mail: info@accessnv.com
Phone: (702) 294-0480
URL: http://www.accessnv.com/

CONNECTUS

Area Codes: 702, 916
e-mail: support@connectus.com
Phone: (702) 323-2008
URL: http://www.connectus.com/

EVERGREEN INTERNET

Area Codes: 303, 602, 702, 801
e-mail: evergreen@enet.net
Phone: (602) 926-4500
URL: http://cybermart.com/

NEVADANET

Area Codes: 702
e-mail: braddlee@nevada.edu
Phone: (702) 784-6861
URL: http://www.scs.unr.edu/

TAHOE ON-LINE
Area Codes: 702, 916
e-mail: support@tol.net
Phone: (702) 588-0616
 URL: http://www.tol.net/

New Hampshire

ADVANCED COMMUNICATION SYSTEMS INC.
Area Codes: 508, 603, 617
e-mail: sales@star.net
Phone: (508) 922-8238
URL: http://www.star.net/

CYBERPORT, LLC
Area Codes: 603
e-mail: info@cyberportal.net
Phone: (603) 542-5833
URL: http://www.cyberportal.net/

EMPIRE.NET, INC.
Area Codes: 508, 603
e-mail: sales@empire.net
Phone: (603) 889-1220
URL: http://www.empire.net/

HARVARDNET
Area Codes: 508, 603, 617
e-mail: whs@harvard.net
Phone: (800) 772-6771
URL: http://harvard.net/

NORTH COUNTRY INTERNET ACCESS
Area Codes: 449, 466, 603, 752
e-mail: ed@moose.ncia.net
Phone: (603) 752-1250
URL: http://www.ncia.net/

New Jersey

ALTERNET - UUNET
Area Codes: 212, 214, 310, 404, 408, 415, 503, 510,
617, 703, 713, 800, 908
e-mail: sales@alter.net
Phone: (800) 488-6384
URL: http://www.alter.net/

NOTES & TIPS

CASTLE NETWORK, INC.
Area Codes: 609, 908
e-mail: request@castle.net
Phone: (800) 577-9449
URL: http://www.castle.net/

NOVASYS INTERACTIVE
Area Codes: 201, 908
e-mail: webdudes@nexxus.novasys.com
Phone: (201) 887-8189
URL: http://www.novasys.com/

TEXEL INTERNATIONAL, INC.
Area Codes: 609, 908
e-mail: info@texel.com
Phone: (908) 297-0290
URL: http://www.texel.com/

WEB EXPRESS
Area Codes: 908
e-mail: info@bw.webex.net
Phone: (908) 704-1826
URL: http://www.webex.net/

New Mexico

COMMUNITY INTERNET ACCESS
Area Codes: 505
e-mail: sysadm@cia-g.com
Phone: (505) 863-2424
URL: http://www.cia-g.com/

INTERNET EXPRESS
Area Codes: 206, 303, 505, 602, 719, 800
e-mail: service@usa.net
Phone: (800) 592-1240
URL: http://www.usa.net/

NEW MEXICO TECHNET, INC.
Area Codes: 505, 520, 800
e-mail: granoff@technet.nm.org
Phone: (505) 345-6555
URL: http://www.nm.org/

WAZOO'S COMPUTERS
Area Codes: 505
e-mail: wazoo@wazoo.com
Phone: (505) 434-5090
URL: http://www.wazoo.com/

ZIANET, INC.
Area Codes: 505
e-mail: webmaster@zianet.com
Phone: (505) 522-1234
URL: http://www.zianet.com/

New York

ACCESS GLOBAL INFORMATION SERVICE INC.
Area Codes: 716
e-mail: paull@ag.net
Phone: (716) 694-5029
URL: http://www.ag.net/

ALBANYNET
Area Codes: 518
e-mail: sales@albany.net
Phone: (518) 462-6262
URL: http://www.albany.net/

ALTERNET - UUNET
Area Codes: 212, 214, 310, 404, 408, 415, 503, 510, 617, 703, 713, 800, 908
e-mail: sales@alter.net
Phone: (800) 488-6384
URL: http://www.alter.net/

SYRACUSE INTERNET
Area Codes: 315
e-mail: mab@vcomm.net
Phone: (315) 233-1948
URL: http://www.vcomm.net/

THOUGHTPORT
Area Codes: 212, 312, 314, 408, 412, 801, 813
e-mail: human@thoughtport.com
Phone: (800) 477-6870
URL: http://www.thoughtport.com/

North Carolina

ALPHANET SOUTH CORPORATION
Area Codes: 910
e-mail: sales@ansouth.net
Phone: (910) 673-3300
URL: http://www.ansouth.net/

INFINET
Area Codes: 202, 301, 410, 703, 804, 910, 919
e-mail: sales@infi.net
Phone: (804) 622-4289
(800) 849-7214
URL: http://www.infi.net/

INTERPATH
Area Codes: 202, 704, 800, 803, 910, 919
e-mail: helpdesk@interpath.net
Phone: (800) 849-6305
URL: http://www.interpath.net/

RED BARN DATA CENTER
Area Codes: 910
e-mail: postmaster@rbdc.rbdc.com
Phone: (910) 774-1600
URL: http://www.rbdc.com/

SUNBELT.NET
Area Codes: 615, 704, 706, 803, 904
e-mail: support@sunbelt.net
Phone: (800) 950-4726
URL: http://www.sunbelt.net/

North Dakota

CORPORATE COMMUNICATIONS
Area Codes: 218, 612, 701
e-mail: dekman@corpcomm.net
Phone: (701) 277-0011
URL: http://www.corpcomm.net/

DAKOTA CENTRAL TELECOMMUNICATIONS COOPERATIVE
Area Codes: 701
e-mail: dwolf@daktel.com
Phone: (701) 652-3184
URL: http://www.daktel.com/

NORTHWESTNET

Area Codes: 206, 208, 360, 406, 503, 509, 701, 907
e-mail: info@nwnet.net
Phone: (206) 562-3000
URL: http://www.nwnet.net/

POLARIS TELCOM

Area Codes: 218, 507, 612, 701
e-mail: info@polaristel.net
Phone: (800) 417-8681
URL: http://www.polaristel.net/

RED RIVER NET

Area Codes: 218, 701
e-mail: lien@rrnet.com
Phone: (701) 232-2227
URL: http://www.rrnet.com/

Ohio

ASCINET

Area Codes: 614
e-mail: info@ascinet.com
Phone: (614) 798-5321
(800) 843-5321
URL: http://www.ascinet.com/

BBS ONE ONLINE SERVICE

Area Codes: 216
e-mail: jeremyc@bbsone.com
Phone: (216) 825-5217
URL: http://www.prgone.com/

DAYTON INTERNET SERVICES, INC.

Area Codes: 513
e-mail: tadams@dayton.net
Phone: (513) 643-0188
URL: http://www.dayton.net/

PRIMENET

Area Codes: 208, 209, 213, 310, 419, 520, 602, 612,
619, 714, 715, 816, 818, 909, 915
e-mail: acctinfo@primenet.com
Phone: (800) 4-NET-FUN
URL: http://www.primenet.com/

APPENDIX A · INTERNET SERVICE PROVIDERS

WINFIELD COMMUNICATION, INC.
Area Codes: 216
e-mail: questions@winc.com
Phone: (216) 867-2904
URL: http://www.winc.com/

Oklahoma

INTERNET OKLAHOMA
Area Codes: 405, 800, 918, 800
e-mail: support@ionet.net
Phone: (405) 721-1580
URL: http://www.ionet.net/

LDS IAMERICA
Area Codes: 210, 214, 318 405, 409, 501, 504 512,
607, 713, 806, 817, 903, 915, 918
e-mail: info@iamerica.net
Phone: (800) 789-4026
URL: http://www.iamerica.net/

MIDNET
Area Codes: 314, 316, 402, 405, 501, 515, 605, 816,
913, 918
e-mail: witts@mid.net
Phone: (800) 682-5550
URL: http://www.mid.net/

OKNET, THE TULSA SUPERNET, BLACK GOLD BBS
Area Codes: 713, 918
e-mail: oksales@oknet.com
Phone: (918) 481-5899
(800) 221-6478
URL: http://www.oknet.com/

VIRTUAL COMMUNITY
Area Codes: 405
e-mail: info@soonernet.com
Phone: (405) 748-6093
URL: http://www.soonernet.com/

Oregon

CENORNET
Area Codes: 503
e-mail: info@cenornet.com
URL: http://www.cenornet.com/

CYBERNET NORTHWEST
Area Codes: 503
e-mail: mgrady@cybernw.com
Phone: (503) 256-5350
URL: http://www.cybernw.com/

DATA RESEARCH GROUP, INC.
Area Codes: 503
e-mail: dklindt@ordata.com
Phone: (503) 465-DATA
URL: http://www.ordata.com/

VASTNET
Area Codes: 503
e-mail: sales@vastnet.com
Phone: (503) 263-0912
URL: http://www.vastnet.com/

WLN INTERNET SERVICES
Area Codes: 206, 360, 503, 509, 800
e-mail: info@wln.com
Phone: (800)-DIALWLN
(360) 923-4000
URL: http://www.wln.com/

Pennsylvania

CHESTER COUNTY INTERNET SERVICES, INC.
Area Codes: 610, 717
e-mail: support@chesco.com
Phone: (610) 857-0505
URL: http://www.chesco.com/

CITYNET, INC.
Area Codes: 412
e-mail: info@city-net.com
Phone: (412) 481-5406
URL: http://www.city-net.com/

COMCAT INC.
Area Codes: 215
e-mail: info@comcat.com
Phone: (215) 230-4923
URL: http://www.comcat.com/

THE NET CONNECTION!
Area Codes: 412
e-mail: sysop@dp.net
Phone: (412) 326-8355
URL: http://www.dp.net/

VOICENET
Area Codes: 215, 302, 609, 610, 800
e-mail: sales@voicenet.com
Phone: (800) 835-5710
URL: http://www.voicenet.com/

Rhode Island

AQUIDNECK WEB INC.
Area Codes: 401, 508
e-mail: info@aqua.net
Phone: (401) 841-5WWW
URL: http://www.aqua.net/

EMI COMMUNICATIONS
Area Codes: 202, 212, 301, 315, 401, 516, 518, 607, 617, 716, 800, 914
e-mail: info@emi.com
Phone: (800) 456-2001
URL: http://www.emi.com/

IDS WORLD NETWORK
Area Codes: 305, 401, 407, 914
e-mail: info@ids.net
Phone: (800) IDS-1680
URL: http://www.ids.net/

PLYMOUTH COMMERCIAL INTERNET EXCHANGE
Area Codes: 401, 508, 617
e-mail: sales@pcix.com
Phone: (617) 741-5900
URL: http://www.pcix.com/

SATURN INTERNET CORPORATION
Area Codes: 401, 617
e-mail: plarkin@saturn.net
Phone: (617) 451-9121
URL: http://www.saturn.net/

South Carolina

CETLINK.NET
Area Codes: 803
e-mail: web-admin@cetlink.net
Phone: (803) 327-2754
URL: http://www.cetlink.net/

GEORGIA BUSINESS NET, INC
Area Codes: 706, 803, 912
e-mail: info@ganet.com
Phone: (706) 823-2115
(800) 201-6349
URL: http://www.ganet.com/

INTERNET CSRA, INC
Area Codes: 706, 803
e-mail: info@csra.net
Phone: (706) 724-1509
URL: http://www.csra.net/

RENAISSANCE INTERACTIVE
Area Codes: 803
e-mail: waycool@ricommunity.com
Phone: (803) 748-0506
URL: http://www.ricommunity.com/

SIMS, INC
Area Codes: 803
e-mail: info@sims.com
Phone: (803) 853-4333
URL: http://www.sims.net/

South Dakota

DAKOTA INTERNET SERVICES, INC.
Area Codes: 605
e-mail: service@dakota.net
Phone: (605) 371-1962
URL: http://www.dakota.net/

APPENDIX A · INTERNET SERVICE PROVIDERS

INTERNET SERVICES OF THE BLACK HILLS, INC.

Area Codes: 605
e-mail: rryan@blackhills.com
Phone: (605) 642-2244

IWAY INTERNET SERVICES

Area Codes: 507, 605
e-mail: gbaar@iw.net
Phone: (605) 331-4211
URL: http://www.iw.net/

MIDNET

Area Codes: 314, 316, 402, 405, 501, 515, 605, 816, 913, 918
e-mail: witts@mid.net
Phone: (800) 682-5550
URL: http://www.mid.net/

RAPIDNET LLC

Area Codes: 605
e-mail: gary@rapidnet.com
Phone: (605) 341-3283
URL: http://www.rapidnet.com/

Tennessee

BLUEGRASSNET

Area Codes: 317, 502, 513, 606, 615, 812
e-mail: sales@bluegrass.net
Phone: (502) 589-INET
URL: http://www.bluegrass.net/

CHATTANOOGA ONLINE

Area Codes: 615
e-mail: support@chattanooga.net
Phone: (615) 267-8867
URL: http://www.chattanooga.net/

PREFERRED INTERNET SERVICES

Area Codes: 615, 703
e-mail: sales@preferred.com
Phone: (615) 323-1142
URL: http://www.preferred.com/pis/

TRI-CITY UNLIMITED (TCU)
Area Codes: 615, 703
e-mail: info@tcu.com
Phone: (615) 279-3377
URL: http://www.tcu.com/

UNITED STATES INTERNET, INC.
Area Codes: 423, 615, 901
e-mail: staff@usit.net
Phone: (800) 218-USIT
URL: http://www.usit.net/

Texas

ACM NETWORK SERVICES
Area Codes: 800, 817
e-mail: account-info@acm.org
Phone: (817) 776-6876
URL: http://www.acm.org/

ALTERNET - UUNET
Area Codes: 212, 214, 310, 404, 408, 415, 503, 510, 617, 703, 713, 800, 908
e-mail: sales@alter.net
Phone: (800) 488-6384
URL: http://www.alter.net/

CHRYSALIS ONLINE SERVICES
Area Codes: 214, 817
e-mail: garry.grosse@chrysalis.org
Phone: (214) 690-9295
(817) 540-5565
URL: http://www.chrysalis.org/

REALLINK, INC.
Area Codes: 512
e-mail: info@reallink.com
Phone: (512) 338-4824
URL: http://www.reallink.com/

ZILKER INTERNET PARK
Area Codes: 512
e-mail: support@zilker.net
Phone: (512) 206-3850
URL: http://www.zilker.net/

APPENDIX A · INTERNET SERVICE PROVIDERS

Utah

AROSNET, INC.
Area Codes: 801
e-mail: info@aros.net
Phone: (801) 532-2767
URL: http://www.aros.net/

I-LINK, INC.
Area Codes: 202, 206, 210, 212, 213, 214, 303, 404, 407, 415, 502, 504, 512, 602, 617, 619, 713, 801
e-mail: support@i-link.net
Phone: (512) 388-2393
(800) 454-6599
URL: http://www.i-link.net/

KDC ON-LINE
Area Codes: 801
e-mail: support@kdcol.com
Phone: (801) 497-9931
URL: http://www.kdcol.com/

LEGACY COMMUNICATIONS, INC.
Area Codes: 801
e-mail: webmaster@lgcy.com
Phone: (801) 521-9257
URL: http://www.lgcy.com/

NOTHING BUT NET
Area Codes: 800, 801
e-mail: info@trey.com
Phone: (801) 535-1801
(800) 951-7226
URL: http://www.trey.com/

Vermont

CENTNET, INC.
Area Codes: 203, 207, 401, 413, 508, 603, 617, 802
e-mail: info@cent.net
Phone: (617) 492-6079
URL: http://www.control.com/centnet/

SOVERNET
Area Codes: 802
e-mail: sales@sover.net
Phone: (802) 463-2111
URL: http://www.sover.net/

TGF TECHNOLOGIES, INC.
Area Codes: 802
e-mail: info@together.org
Human e-mail: helpdesk@together.org
Phone: (802) 862-2030
URL: http://www.together.com/

Virginia

AHOYNET INFORMATION SERVICES
Area Codes: 540, 703, 804
e-mail: captain@ahoynet.com
Phone: (540) 720-4048
URL: http://www.ahoynet.com/

CAPITAL AREA INTERNET SERVICE
Area Codes: 202, 301, 410, 703
e-mail: support@cais.com
Phone: (703) 448-4470
URL: http://www.cais.com/

DATABANK, INC.
Area Codes: 202, 301, 316, 703, 800, 816, 913, 914
e-mail: support@databank.com
Phone: (913) 842-6699
URL: http://www.databank.com/

DIGITAL EXPRESS GROUP - DIGEX(TM)
Area Codes: 201, 202, 212, 215, 301, 302, 410, 412,
516, 609, 610, 703, 718, 804, 908, 914, 917
e-mail: sales@digex.net
Phone: (800) 969-9090
(301) 847-5000
URL: http://www.digex.net/

VISIONARY COMMUNICATIONS
Area code: 307
e-mail: info@vcn.com
Phone: (307) 682-1884
URL: http://www.vcn.com/

Washington

ACCESSONE
Area Codes: 206, 360, 509
e-mail: info@accessone.com
Phone: (206) 827-5344
URL: http://www.accessone.com/

INTERNET EXPRESS
Area Codes: 206, 303, 505, 602, 719, 800
e-mail: service@usa.net
Phone: (800) 592-1240
(719) 592-1240
URL: http://www.usa.net/

ISOMEDIA.COM
Area Codes: 206
e-mail: platinum@isomedia.com
Phone: (206) 881-8769
URL: http://www.isomedia.com/

SERVNET
Area Codes: 206
e-mail: admin@serv.net
Phone: (206) 789-4155
URL: http://www.serv.net/

VISUAL INTERNET SERVICES GROUP
Area Codes: 206, 360
e-mail: visual@oz.net
Phone: (206) 946-9426
URL: http://www.oz.net/~visual/

West Virginia

CITYNET CORPORATION
Area Codes: 304
e-mail: support@citynet.net
Phone: (304) 342-5700
URL: http://www.citynet.net/

INTREPID TECHNOLOGIES, INC.
Area Codes: 304
e-mail: support@intrepid.net
Phone: (304) 876-1199
URL: http://www.intrepid.net/

MOUNTAINNET, INC.
Area Codes: 304
e-mail: info@mountain.net
Phone: (304) 594-9075
(800) 846-1458
URL: http://www.mountain.net/

NETCOM ON-LINE COMMUNICATION SERVICES, INC.
Area Codes: 304
e-mail: info@netcom.com
Phone: (408) 983-5950
(800) 353-6600
URL: http://www.netcom.com/

RAM TECHNOLOGIES
Area Codes: 304, 606, 614,
e-mail: sales@ramlink.net
Phone: (800) 950-8878
URL: http://www.ramlink.net/

Wisconsin

ATHENET
Area Codes: 414
e-mail: athenet@athenet.net
Phone: (414) 954-0376
URL: http://www.athenet.net/

AXIS.NET, INC.
Area Codes: 414
e-mail: nl@axisnet.com
Phone: (414) 290-2947
URL: http://www.axisnet.com/

BOSSNET INTERNET SERVICES
Area Codes: 608, 815
e-mail: mbusam@bossnt.com
Phone: (608) 362-1340
(800) 475-1872
URL: http://www.bossnt.com/

COMPUTIZE
Area Codes: 210, 214, 414, 512, 708, 713
e-mail: support@computize.com
Phone: (713) 613-4800
URL: http://www.domi.net/

APPENDIX A · INTERNET SERVICE PROVIDERS

EXCEL.NET
Area Codes: 414
e-mail: manager@excel.net
Phone: (414) 452-0455
URL: http://www.excel.net/

Wyoming

COFFEYNET
Area Codes: 307
e-mail: web@coffey.com
Phone: (307) 234-5443
URL: http://www.coffey.com/

NETCONNECT
Area Codes: 307, 801
e-mail: office@tcd.net
Phone: (307) 789-8001
(800) 689-8001
URL: http://www.tcd.net/

WAVE COMMUNICATIONS INC.
Area Codes: 307
e-mail: jack@wave.sheridan.wy.us
Phone: (307) 674-4925
URL: http://wave.sheridan.wy.us/index.html/

WYOMING.COM LLC
Area Codes: 307
e-mail: info@wyoming.com
Phone: (307) 332-3030
(800) WYO-INET
URL: http://www.wyoming.com/

APPENDIX B

CAUTION: Children at Play

There is indeed a world of insalubrious content being bought, sold, and given away through cyberspace. However, publicized cases of harm or potential harm to children often fail to mention that those who are most vulnerable spend hours of unsupervised, unregulated time online—an activity about as safe as letting your pre-teen kids hang out alone at the local video arcade after dark.

So, outside of waiting for legislation to protect families online (though some would question the wisdom of seeking additional federal regulations for any purpose), what can be done? Currently, there are two main devices available to help the homeschool parent monitor and protect their children while using the Internet: 1) Common sense, and 2) Software programs which filter out undesirable content and prevent access to unsavory sites.

COMMON-SENSE DEFENSES

Believe it or not, the Internet is currently safer to surf than the closest beach at the busiest time of year. The reason? While people can and will approach you and your children in public places in real life (IRL), it is highly unlikely that you will receive unsolicited interruptions while online. Wackos will not come search you out, unless you go to the places where wackos hang out. It would be impossible to list all of these electronic holes-in-the-wall, and it is not necessary. The virtual billboards and neon signs say it all. Just as you would not drop off your children for an unchaperoned stroll down Broadway or Main Street in most larger cities, you should not drop your children off for an unsupervised, undirected period of "surfing" the net.

Don't panic! It's really not as scary as it sounds, if you follow a few practical guidelines:

1. Have a specific purpose for being online, and monitor the online activity for meeting those objectives. Allow for certain freedom in pursuing related links and searches—but if necessary, bookmark (save the address in your hotlist) those sites for later investigation, and return to the goal at hand.

2. Set a time limit. As with other visual electronic media such as TV, videos, or computer games, it is easy to become absorbed in work or play to the exclusion of all else. Use your computer's built-in clock to keep track of time, or set a wind-up kitchen timer, if necessary, as a reminder to take a break.

3. Children should not engage in unsupervised "chat" with strangers while online. While it is true that people of any age can pose as children while in children's areas, the more common danger is simply "schoolyard chatter" that can be meaningless or unwholesome. Parents should be instrumental in setting up electronic pen-pals with other parents.

4. Keep personal information private. Unless you or your children know who they are talking to and have a valid reason (and permission) to do so, instruct them not to post (type online) confidential information such as your home telephone number, street address, credit card info, or other personal data.

5. Maintain the moral standards and character-building guidelines that you enforce in real life. Explain that just because you have the capability to go anywhere online, doesn't mean you should. Watch the roadsigns! Turn away from addresses and buttons that suggest or indicate they lead to violent (i.e. destructive games), pornographic, or occult sites.

The bottom line, as with the real world, is that you cannot always police your children; nor should you have to, if they are adequately prepared and trained. If you can trust your children to exhibit high standards in public when you are not present, then you should also be able to trust them online. If your children are unable to police themselves online with your guidance and instruction, however, then you are likely having difficulty with respect and obedience in other areas.

FILTERING & SCREENING SOFTWARE

While the term "censorware" likely reveals the originator's philosophy regarding the first amendment, the word has caught on as a classification of a new breed of Internet software. Such programs enable parents to actively or passively restrict or control access to specific types of content, based on one or more of the following criteria:

1. The software may be linked to a list of restricted sites maintained by the software publisher and made available to registered users for a nominal extra charge.

2. The software may maintain separate user profiles for each family member, with unique access privileges and passcodes for each user. The software may allow parents to add specific sites to the list of inaccessible addresses.

3. The software may support third-party ratings evaluations, such as those from a group of CD-ROM and video game publishers called RSACi (Recreational Software Advisory Council), and SafeSurf (a group formed in 1995 by parents wishing to create a "child safe" environment on the Internet).

4. The software may filter some or all of the following types of incoming information: Web sites, Newsgroups, and chat rooms. It may also allow blocking of specific outgoing information as typed in by the parent, or administrator—such as phone numbers and addresses.

On the surface, these filtering programs sound like a good idea—or even necessary to ensure a pure environment for the home; but it is the author's opinion that they are, for the most part, based on faulty reasoning. Here's why:

1) While these programs do indeed work on filtering some of the content most of the time, none of them will filter all content all of the time.

2) Private ratings systems are incomplete, and based on someone else's judgment, not the parents. Plus, they generally make you pay for updates.

3) Public ratings systems like RSACi and SafeSurf

are entirely voluntary, and even if stringently applied, are still based on relatively low, if any, moral standards—just like the movie industry's rating system.

4) Some of the programs screen content based on rating factors such as nudity, profanity, and homosexuality on a scale of 1 to 10. Such a scheme assumes (incorrectly, we believe) that ANY such content is acceptable in a family environment. The RASCi ratings for nudity, for example, begin at level 1: "revealing attire," and progresses to level 4, "provocative frontal nudity." Contrary to the underlying philosophy of these rating systems, pornography is not "adult" content that gradually or suddenly becomes acceptable when children turn 18 or 21. Similarly, it seems ludicrous for younger children to be safe using or being exposed to "mild expletives," while your teenagers can advance to "strong, vulgar language" and then graduate to "crude or explicit references." It is incredible that these faulty assumptions underlly all of the ratings systems.

5) A few programs also attempt to monitor such intangible factors as "bigotry" and "intolerance." While we presume the primary target of these "censorship" controls is to eliminate racial predjudice and violence, could they not also be used to thwart conservative politics or Christian causes, if the database administrator or software publisher deemed certain religious or political sites guilty of "intolerance?"

BACK TO REALITY

The packaging of these programs seems to capitalize on parent's fear that their children will "accidently" run across unacceptable content. While this is certainly possible, it is not probable. Without any screening software installed, navigation on the Internet requires that all buttons, addresses, and key words have to be read, typed in, and clicked in order to access a desired link. These are activities requiring conscious choice—not an accidental slip.

The fact is, however, that none of the programs on the market are secure against children or adults that wish to thwart the intended security measures. For example, getting around passcode protection could be as easy as downloading an alternate web browser with which to gain unrestricted access. Forbidden words, phrases, or information—if a child was determined to provide it or say it—could be typed in with spaces between the letters, thus going undetected by the computer's "checker."

The best protection, by far, is teaching children to be responsible and accountable for their actions online, just as they are in real life. While some people of any age may pretend to live in a fantasy world through virtual identities in cyberspace, no one can hide from the Maker of man and Creator of the universe. When the electricity fails, reality prevails. Remember to teach your children that the online world—although a fantastic realm—is an artificial universe that ceases to exist when the power goes out. Only the light of God's truth is everlasting.

MANUFACTURERS OF SCREENING SOFTWARE

INTERGO COMMUNICATIONS INC.
InterGo 2.1
http://www.intergo.com
(214) 424-7882
Windows 3.1, Windows 95
$49.95

MICROSYSTEMS SOFTWARE
Cyber Patrol 3.0
http://www.microsys.com/cyber/
(800) 828-2608
Windows 3.1, Windows 95
$29.95 (plus updates)

NET NANNY, LTD.
Net Nanny 2.1
http://www.netnanny.com
(800) 340-7177
Windows 3.1, Windows 95
$39.95

NET SHEPHERD INC.
Net Shepherd 1.0
http://www.shepherd.net
(403) 250-5310
DOS, Windows 3.1, Windows 95
Free

NOTES & TIPS

✔ *As a reminder to be careful online, you may find it helpful and encouraging to attach some relevant scripture verses on or around your computer screen, such as Phillipians 4:8 and others.*

NEWVIEW INC.
Specs for Kids
http://www.newview.com
no phone
Windows 3.1, Windows 95
Free

SPYGLASS INC.
SurfWatch
http://www.surfwatch.com
(800) 458-6600
Windows 3.1, Windows 95
$49.00

SOLID OAK SOFTWARE, INC.
Cybersitter 2.1
http://www.solidoak.com
(800) 388-2761)
Mac, Windows 3.1, Windows 95
$39.95

Guide to Plug-Ins for the World Wide Web

You've probably heard about all the great things that the Internet can do—particularly through the World Wide Web. You've also probably wondered, "Why can't my computer do that? Do I need a new system?"

While it is true that most of the latest technological advances on the Web require a faster chip, plenty of RAM, and a 28.8 modem, read on before you dump your current model or give up hope. With some experimentation (and more than some patience) you too can successfully install and use plug-ins. Once you do, prepare to be both amazed and amused—sometimes because the result is suprising or exciting, and sometimes because it's simply ridiculous that you spent so much time just to see another spinning logo.

WHAT'S A PLUG-IN?

A plug-in is to your Web browser what a system extension is to your system software. It adds functionality and capability to your Web-viewing application that enables it to receive and manipulate other types of media or data. Some popular plug-ins enable you to listen to live radio broadcast, participate in a chat room conversation with your voice instead of the keyboard, or watch video clips without waiting for them to download.

Most plug-ins are being used to simply provide added entertainment value, but a few also offer practical enhancements to Web site functionality. There are about 100 or so plug-ins currently available for Netscape and Netscape-compatible browsers. The rapid development and integration of plug-ins is quite amazing, considering that the very first one—called ShockWave—was made available in 1995.

While plug-ins are the latest technological marvel to hit the Web, they are relatively immature when it comes to reliability and compatibility. The day is quickly arriving, however, when these special programs will be completely integrated into your computer's operating system (Microsoft's plan) or when the browser itself becomes an operating system (Netscape's intention). Both company's goals will increase performance and reliability of advanced Web site features, which will help transform the Internet into a powerful, intuitive, interactive delivery system. Until that time, you may enjoy exploring a few of the most popular plug-ins and the Web sites that use them.

HOW TO INSTALL PLUG-INS

For Windows Users

1) Type in the URL to access the publisher's web site, then click on links which guide you to download the appropriate version for your computer. You will need to choose a directory for the download (the default is the directory where your browser is located).

2) Most files download as an .EXE file. Use File Manager or Windows Explorer to locate the file, then double-click on it to launch the installer. The installer will locate the Netscape Navigator program on your hard drive, and will ask you to choose a directory in which the plug-in will reside.

3) Click "Yes" to the question regarding placement of the plug-in icon in the Program Manager, in order to see at a glance all the plug-ins you've installed.

4) If Netscape is still open, quit and then re-launch the program. After restarting, go the the "Help" menu and select "About Plug-ins" to double-check that your installation was successful (you'll see all of the plug-ins listed there).

5) With your browser open, select "Load URL" and then type in an address which utilizes the new plug-in. In most cases, you can simply return to the manufacturer's web site (tip: save it in your hotlist) for updated links to sites that use the plug-in features.

For Macintosh Users

1) Type in the URL to access a publisher's web site from the list below, then click on links which guide you to <u>download</u> the appropriate version for your computer. Be careful to choose either PPC (PowerPC) for newer models, or 68K for older models. The file will automatically download into Netscape's default directory, or you may create an alternate download directory by selecting the folowing menus: "Options, General Preferences, Applications, Browse."

2) When the download is complete, the plug-in file will automatically expand if you have compression software installed, and Netscape is already configured to use it as a helper application. We recommend Stuffit Expander, which you can download from ftp://ftp.ncsa.uiuc.edu/Mosaic/Mac/Helpers/stuffit-expander-352.hqx. To configure Netscape to automatically recognize and unstuff ".hqx" (compressed) files, select the following menus: "Options, General Preferences, Helpers," then click on Stuffit Expander for "Macintosh Binaries."

3) Go to your downloads folder (generally inside the Netscape folder) and open it. You will usually find a new folder containing the downloaded plug-in and associated Read-Me files. If there is no folder, or if the plug-in did not expand automatically, then double-click on the .hqx file now (be sure you have Stuffit Expander installed first). After locating the actual plug-in file itself, drag it to the same folder that contains the Netscape application.

4) If Navigator is still running, quit the program, and then restart it. To check whether the plug-in is now recognized by the browser, go to the Apple menu and select "About Plug-ins" to view the list of installed applications.

5) With your browser open, select "Load URL" and then type in an address which utilizes the new plug-in. In most cases, you can simply return to the manufacturer's web site (tip: save it in your hotlist) for updated links to sites that use the plug-in features.

25 MOST POPULAR PLUG-INS

Here are 25 browser programs to get you started, listed alphabetically by name. Beneath the name is the purpose for the plug-in, followed by the publisher, the Web address to visit for downloading, and the platform/OS required to use the plug-in.

ADOBE ACROBAT 3.0
PDF (Portable Document Format) Viewer by Adobe
http://www.adobe.com/acrobat/3beta/main.html#dl
Win3.1, Win95, WinNT, Mac 68K, Mac PPC

ACTIVE X
ActiveX Enabler for Netscape by Ncompass
http://www.ncompasslabs.com/products.htm
Win3.1, Win95, WinNT

ARGUS MAP VIEWER
Dynamic Map Viewer by Argus Technologies
http://www.argusmap.com/
Win3.1, Win95, WinNT

ASTOUND WEB PLAYER
Presentation Player by Gold Disk
http://www.golddisk.com
Win3.1, Win95

CARBON COPY
Desktop Takeover Utility by MicroCom
http://www.microcom.com/cc/ccdnload.htm
Win3.1, Win95

CONCERTO
Form Enabler by Alpha Software
http://www.alphasoftware.com/concerto/
Win95

COOL FUSION
Streamed AVI Movie Viewer
http://www.webber.iterated.com/
Win95

✔ *Most plug-ins may be downloaded free of charge; however, many publishers ask for basic registration information in exchange—which helps them further evaluate and develop their product.*

CRESCENDO!

MIDI File Player by LiveUpdate

http://www.liveupdate.com
Win3.1, Win95, Mac 68K, Mac PPC

CYBERSPELL

Online Spelling Checker by Inso Corporation

http://www.inso.com/
Win3.1, Win95, WinNT

EARTHTIME

Time Zone Viewer by Starfish Software

http://www.starfishsoftware.com/getearth.html
Win95, WinNT

FRACTAL VIEWER

Zoomable Image Viewer by Iterated Systems

http://www.interated.com/fracview/fv_home.htm
Win3.1, Win95

HINDSITE

Surfing Activity Indexer by ISYS/Odyssey Development Inc.

http://www.isysev.com/
Win3.1, Win95, WinNT

HISTORY TREE

Web Activity Mapper by SmartBrowser

http://www.smartbrowser.com/
Win3.1, Win 95

ICHAT

Real-time Chat Enabler by ichat

http://www.ichat.com/ichat2/download.html
Win3.1, Win95, Mac 68K, Mac PPC

LIGHTNING STRIKE

High-Compression Image Viewer by Infinop

http://www.infinop.com/html/infinop.html
Win3.1, Win95, WinNT, Mac 68K, Mac PPC, Unix

LOOK@ME

Remote Desktop Viewer

http://www.farallon.com/
Win3.1, Win95, WinNT, Mac 68K, Mac PPC

When browsing the Web, and especially during downloading files, we suggest closing all other applications that may be running in the background. Unless you have tons of RAM (16MB or better), Netscape and other Web browsers may crash or freeze while other programs are running, due to memory conflicts.

APPENDIX C · GUIDE TO PLUG-INS FOR THE WWW

mBED

Interactive Multimedia Animation

http://www.mbed.com/
Win3.1, Win95, WinNT, Mac 68K, Mac PPC

MOVIESTAR

QuickTime Movie Viewer by Intelligence At Large

http://www.beingthere.com/moviestar/plugins/movies-tar.html
Win3.1, Win95, Mac 68K, Mac PPC

NET-INSTALL

File Transfer Solution by 20/20 Software

http://www.twenty.com/Pages/NINIPI.shtml
Win3.1, Win95, WinNT

PENOP

Electronic Signature Enabler by PenOp, Inc.

http://www.penop.com/
Win95, WinNT

POINTCAST NETWORK

Network News Receiver by PointCast

http://www.pointcast.com/cgi-bin/download.pl
Win3.1, Win95

REALAUDIO

Streamed Audio Player by Progressive Networks

http://www.realaudio.com/products/player2.0.html
Win3.1, Win95, WinNT, Mac 68K, Mac PPC, Unix

SHOCKTALK

Speech Recognition by Digital Dreams

http://www.surftalk.com/
Macintosh 68K, Macintosh PPC

SHOCKWAVE FOR DIRECTOR

Multimedia Player by Macromedia

http://www.macromedia.com/Tools/Shockwave/
Win3.1, Win95, Mac 68K, Mac PPC

SIZZLER

Streamed Animation by Totally Hip Software

http://www.totallyhip.com/
Win3.1, Win95, Mac 68K, Mac PPC

APPENDIX D

Guide to Online Academies

For home educators the Internet can play an important role in gathering educationonal materials and networking with other homeschool families without leaving home. There is an ever expanding array of distance learning resources online–especially on the Web. Here are some places to explore to help you on your home study journey.

CENTER FOR EDUCATION REFORM
Information about "Charter Schools" and what they offer.

http://edreform.com/charters.htm

***

HOMESCHOOL WORLD
Bill and Mary Pride's Web site will soon be offering: "Academy of the Future (TM)" Directory of K-12 online courses, plus courses to be offered by us through this web site. "University of the Future (TM)" Directory of college and graduate level online courses, plus courses to be offered by us through this web site. "Web School (TM)" Lesson plans including links to other educational sites on the web. Check back often to take advantage of these wonderful resources as soon as they are available!

http://www.home-school.com/

***

INSTITUTE FOR THE STUDY OF THE LIBERAL ARTS AND SCIENCE
The Institute for Study of the Liberal Arts (ISLA) was founded in 1993 primarily to sponsor the publication of a classical children's journal called Hereditas. In May of 1995, the ISLA created Scholars' Online Academy to support homeschooling

parents who are coping with the difficulties of high school, thus becoming the ISLAS (Institute for Study of the Liberal Arts and Sciences).

http://www.ictheweb.com/islas/

✳✳✳

CALVERT SCHOOL'S HOME PAGE

"Thank you for your interest in Calvert School's Home Instruction Department. An outgrowth of our prestigious Day School in Baltimore, Maryland, our home study courses have been used to educate hundreds of thousands of children since its inception in 1906."

http://www.jhu.edu/~calvert/

✳✳✳

WELCOME TO THE HOME EDUCATION RESOURCES CENTER CATALOG.

HERC offers a variety of educational materials to help your children learn. Included are textbooks and core course materials for teachers and homeschoolers as well as drills and fun projects that the whole family can enjoy.

http://www.cts.com/~netsales/herc/herccat.html

✳✳✳

LAUREL SPRINGS SCHOOL

A tradition in independent study, dedicated to providing online and homeschooling to K-12 children.

http://www.laurelsprings.com/

✳✳✳

PEARBLOSSOM PRIVATE SCHOOL, INC.

A private school program for K-12 students done from home.

http://www.vcnet.com/bbd/pps/pps.htm

✳✳✳

FRASER VALLEY DISTANCE EDUCATION SCHOOL

FVDES is a distance educational facility offering support and materials to those who homeschool.

http://www.fvrcs.gov.bc.ca/

✳✳✳

INSTITUTE FOR DISTANCE EDUCATION

IDE was created by the chancellor of the University of Maryland System in 1990 in response to recommendations of the UMS Task Force on Distance Education. The institute coordinates and facilitates the growth of distance education capabilities within UMS.

http://www.umuc.edu/ide/ide.html

✳✳✳

CHRYSALIS SCHOOL

An independent study program for students of all ages. Students meet weekly with their teachers for home assignments in the required subject areas. Assignments are individualized and based on the student's needs, interests, and abilities.

http://www.wolfe.net/~chrysali/

✳✳✳

CLASSROOM CONNECT

It is a resource that will help you locate some of the most interesting and useful information that is available to K12 educators online.

http://www.classroom.net/classroom/info.html

✳✳✳

THE MICHIGAN INFORMATION TECHNOLOGY NETWORK

MITN is a non-profit organization whose mission is to improve access to education through distance education technologies serving the best interests of Michigan businesses, schools and citizens.

http://www.mitn.msu.edu?/

✳✳✳

SATELLITE EDUCATIONAL RESOURCES CONSORTIUM (SERC)

You've opened the window to a world of learning resources that might otherwise be unavailable. With SERC programs, students can join thousands of others around the U. S. to participate in courses outside their regular school curriculum.

http://www.scsn.net/~serc/

✳✳✳

CYBERSCHOOL

Eugene Public School District 4J in Eugene, Oregon USA announces the opening of CyberSchool, its Internet based distance learning program offering high school credit courses to students around the world. Students must have an email account and access to the World Wide Web through a multimedia browser such as Netscape Navigator or Microsoft Explorer. Classes are $300 (US) for a full semester length course. Some shorter courses are also available.

http://CyberSchool.4j.lane.edu

✳✳✳

QUEST! HOME OF NASA'S K-12 INTERNET INITIATIVE

Their mission: To provide support and services for schools, teachers and students to fully utilize the Internet, and its underlying information technologies, as a basic learning tool.

http://quest.arc.nasa.gov/

✳✳✳

GLOBAL NETWORK ACADEMY

A global non-profit organization, intends to improve education by helping students find online and distance education courses and programs through their online course catalog.

http://uu-gna.mit.edu:8001/uu-gna/

✳✳✳

HOMESCHOOL RESOURCE CENTER

Provides information on their "Homeschool Academy", with many other resources including legal tips with a product catalog as well.

http://www.primenet.com/~elvis/home/home.html

✳✳✳

Glossary

Here are some terms that you will encounter as a result of your online adventures. As strange as it may seem to you now, you will soon become conversant with many of these words. Not all of these words are used in *Homeschool Guide to The Internet*, but have been included for your reference, should you get stumped and don't wish to appear ignorant. (You may also use this list to impress your friends, family, and neighbors with your new vocabulary.)

AOL
Abbreviation for "America Online."

ASCII
Acronym for "American Standard for Computer Information Interchange" or "American Standard Code for Information Interchange." ASCII is the standard code representing all combinations of keyboard characters for computers around the world.

BOOKMARKS
A feature on Web browsers that lets you store the addresses of Web sites you plan to visit frequently. Also know as "hotlists" in some Web browsers.

BPS
Abbreviation for "Bits Per Second," a measurement of the data transmission speed for modems. Sometimes synonymous with "Baud Rate." A "14.4 modem" can move 14,400 bits per second.

BROWSER
Software designed specifically to navigate the World Wide Web, display HyperText Markup Language (HTML) documents, and manage the transmission and downloading of files and information.

BULLETIN BOARD SYSTEM (BBS)
The predecessor to today's modern Internet Service Provider. AOL and CompuServe are examples of "hyper-BBS" systems that have added Internet functions. The content of many older bulletin boards is now on the Internet.

CHAT ROOMS

A live area inside an online service where subscribers can talk to each other on a variety of subjects, or simply watch others interact. Chat rooms can be either public or private.

CIS

Abbreviation for "Compuserve Information Service."

CYBERSPACE

A slang reference to the online universe.

DOMAIN

Consists of the "name"and "type." The name makes the address the computer sees into an address recognizable to the user. The type refers to the type of organization such as org., gov., or com..

DOWNLOAD

The transfer of programs or files from a remote computer to your personal computer (usually stored on the internal drive of your PC).

E-MAIL

Short for "Electronic Mail." Refers to a variety of services and methods by which you can send private and public messages electronically.

EMOTICON

Combining "emotion" with "icon." Also known as "smileys." A sideways smile created with standard keyboard characters. (See Appendix D)

FAQ

(Frequently Asked Questions) -- FAQs are documents that list and answer the most common questions on a particular subject.

FLAME

Sending messages of an inflammatory nature ito a fellow cyber-surfer is known as "flaming."

FINGER

A "Unix" command that enables a person to request to see information about another user on the Internet.

FORUM

An area of an online service set aside for posting ideas and comments, and responding to requests for information and posts from other subscribers. Forums, much like special-interest bulletin boards, are established by topic and subtopic.

FTP
Abbreviation for "File Transfer Protocol." The standard procedure by which files are transferred from one computer to another over the Internet, including text, sound, video, graphics, and programs.

GIF
Acronym for "Graphic Interchange Format," a type of graphic image stored in a form that can be read by most computer platforms.

GOPHER
A feature of the Internet that allows you to browse huge amounts of information. Refers to the manner in which the program "goes for" specific information in a mountain of data. Originated at the University of Minnesota, where the school mascot is the golden gopher.

HOME PAGE
A location or site on the World Wide Web. The word "page" is really a misnomer, as a Web site can be comprised of many actual pages.

HOTLIST
A user's list of most visited sites on the WWW. Like an address book (also known as "bookmarks" in some browsers).

HTML
Abbreviation for "HyperText Markup Language." A language or format used for creating hypertext documents on the World Wide Web, similar to style tags or script programming.

HTTP
HyperText Transfer Protocol. An information retrieval mechanism for HTML documents.

HYPERGRAPHIC
A graphic image that acts as a button to link the user with more information or some predefined event (sound, movie, etc.).

HYPERLINK
The underlying connection that is programmed into a highlighted area of text, graphic, or button to respond to user input, such as a mouse click, to transport the user to another location, or cause a predefined event to happen such as a sound, movie, etc.

GLOSSARY

HYPERMEDIA
Any form of information, such as text or graphics, that is programmed to interact with the user.

HYPERTEXT
A link to other documents containing more information on the same or a related topic. These are often identified as different colored text with an underline, which may be clicked on to activate.

INTERNET
An expansive, worldwide collection of millions of interconnected computers and computer networks.

ISP
Abbreviation for "Internet Service Provider," a company that can provide computer users with access to the Internet, usually for a monthly fee and hourly usage charge.

JPEG
Stands for Joint Photographic Experts Group and is a standard for compressing graphic images.

KEYWORD
A specified word or phrase designated to be used with ISP's, Online Services or other forums to access the desired areas.

LINK
A connection from one World Wide Web page to another. Links are usually highlighted in a different color, or underlined.

MB
Abbreviation for "MegaBytes" which is a unit of measure for computer memory (RAM) and hard drive capacity (storage space). 1 MB is equal to 1,000 K, or exactly 1,048,576 bytes of data.

MODEM
A term formed from combining the words "modulate" with "demodulate" in reference to the way in which the device processes data signals for transmission over telephone lines.

NET
Short form of "Internet." See "Internet."

NEWBIE
Common online reference to a newcomer.

NEWSGROUP
A forum on "Usenet" where users with common interests can gather online to discuss questions and post comments.

ONLINE
A reference to computer services accessed by modems utilizing telephone lines. Also, the state of using these services as opposed to being "offline."

OS
Abbreviation for "Operating System," the software that loads into memory when a computer starts. The OS provides a unique environment that defines how the computer looks and behaves.

PC
Although these two letters have become synonymous with IBM-compatible computers, it is simply an abbreviation for any make or model of "personal computer."

POST
The act of creating and putting a message, program, or file online. Also, a message in a bulletin board or forum.

PPP
Point-to-Point Protocol. A protocol used for direct dial-up Internet connections. PPP is a newer, slightly better version of SLIP.

RAM
Acronym for "Random Access Memory." The most common type of RAM is used by your computer's central processing unit (CPU) to store instructions and data loaded by the software you are currently running.

SESSION
The period or length of time spent online, from sign-on to sign-off.

SERVER
A host computer that manages communication links, file transfer, and stores Web pages and data libraries.

SLIP
Serial-line Internet working protocol. A serial line being a telephone line, SLIP is a connection to the Internet through a phone line. Often used synonymously with PPP.

SNAIL MAIL
A common online reference to mail sent via traditional channels, such as the U.S. Postal Service.

GLOSSARY

TCP/IP
An acronym for "Transmission Control Protocol/Internet Protocol," the protocol language that Internet machines use to communicate.

TELNET
The program used to login from one Internet site to another.

THREAD
A specific series of posts or articles in a forum or newsgroup all pertaining to one certain topic.

UPLOAD
The process of transmitting files from your computer to remote computer such as a bulletin board, online service, or Web server.

URL (UNIFORM RESOURCE LOCATOR)
The address for each Web page or site. Because there are millions of them they are lengthy and specific.

USENET
A world-wide system of discussion groups or newsgroups. There are loads of newsgroups each on a different topic.

V.32bis
The data compression standard for 14.4 kbps modems.

V.34bis
The data compression standard for 28.8 kbps modems.

WAIS
Acronym for "Wide Area Information Server." Pronounced "wayz." A database that allows you to search through vast amounts of information on the Internet. Contains special-interest topics and indexes.

WWW
The "World Wide Web!" is a network of computers tied together by telephone communications which provides access to information around the globe.

About My Mom & Dad...

MARK & WENDY DINSMORE

Mark's first computer was an Apple II+ that he bought in 1982 for $2,275 with four years of savings from working part time. The then state of the art PC came with a whopping 48K of RAM. Today, Mark wonders how he can get by with less than 48MB of RAM—equivalent to 1,000 Apple II+ systems!

Dad, can I have the keys to the computer?

Mark's interest in programming led him to the CIS (Computer Information Systems) program at Christian Heritage College in San Diego, California. He graduated with a B.S. in Business Administration. He has worked in marketing, design, and product development for several Christian publishers, and has been involved in the homeschooling industry for nearly a decade. Mark currently serves as Creative Director at Great Christian Books in Elkton, Maryland, where he lives with his wife and son.

Wendy cut her computing teeth on the venerable TRS-80 "supercomputer," fondly recalled by many as the "trash-80" personal computer. Descended from a line of IBM employees, Wendy did not graduate (some may say "defect") to the Macintosh camp until 1988, when both she and Mark used a "powerful" (TIC) Macintosh Plus with 1MB RAM, and drove 40 miles round trip for "hi-res" 300 dpi laser copies.

Today, Wendy also spends her share of time in front of the computer screen; during the day as a desktop publishing work-at-home mom (also for Great Christian Books) and at night as the Dinsmore's resident online expert. Both Mark and Wendy are active in homeschooling their preschool son, Garrison, whose favorite learning experience is working next to Mom on his own computer.

WE'D LOVE TO HEAR FROM YOU!

*We hope that the **Homeschool Guide** has gotten you off to a great start as you take the on-ramp to the Information Superhighway. Because the online world is an ever-growing and changing universe, there may be new or different things you've discovered along your journey that would make **Homeschool Guide** a better tool for all who read it. Do you have questions that weren't answered? Resources that should be added or changed? Drop us a note. Your feedback is welcome! And while you're surfing, visit our home page. See you on the Web!*

e-mail: hsguide@ssnet.com • URL: http://www.ssnet.com/~hsguide.online.html